What's Important:

Understanding and Working with Values Perspectives

What's Important:
Understanding and Working with Values Perspectives

Kenton Hyatt, Ph.D.
Cheryl De Ciantis, Ph.D.

Integral Publishers
Tucson, Arizona

Integral Publishers
1418 N. Jefferson Ave.
Tucson, AZ 85712

Cover photography by Kenton Hyatt.

Cover design by Jeannie Carlisle.

ISBN: 978-0-9896827-5-6

To four people who are truly living their values,
Abraham Hyatt, Rose Hyatt Bowcut, Laurel Hyatt Blair, Willow Hyatt,
to their wonderful partners,
and to the amazing people they are raising
to understand and live their own values

Table of Contents

ACKNOWLEDGEMENTS

We are grateful for the mentoring and years-long friendship of Brian Hall and Benjamin "Father Benny" Tonna, who built a remarkable edifice which is still foundational for all future values work. Others to whom we owe thanks for ongoing insights into values and for their significant support of our work include Elva Castaneda de Hall, Mike Munro Turner, Scott Bristol, Steven Phillips, Ginger Grant, Fehrunnisa and Jim Moore, Gary Merrill, Carine Dartiguepeyrou, Michel Saloff-Coste, Donna Montgomery, Kjersti Johanne Steinskog, Arne Sverre Modahl, Robert Thomas, Terry Blum, Frank Melis, Robert Burnside, Rebecca Henson, Joyce Richman, Donna Riechmann, Martha Tilyard, Geoff Grenert, Julie Johnson, Didier Gonin, Pamela Mayer, and Michael Ray. Special thanks to Russ Volckmann and Jeannie Carlisle, who are both deeply knowledgeable and deeply generous. Special thanks also to Phil Harrington, who gave the online Values Perspectives survey its clean look and a functionality of persisting elegance, and to Ollie Armstrong, who has our back.

Preface

For years, as we have introduced and described values and how to understand their assessment, two responses kept recurring. The first is some version of, "Wow. This is profound and powerful. Now I really understand what is happening." The second is something like, "This is great, but I'm overwhelmed. This is just too much to try and keep track of." In large part, our reason for writing this book is to address those two responses. People are used to the idea of working with behaviors, but values can seem intangible. Yet values are more powerful in daily life than most people consciously recognize. Even when we do acknowledge the power of values, it is hard to know what exactly to do both about them and with them. Our intent is to provide a handbook for understanding and working with values.

Our work with values reaches back to the 1970s, when the idea of studying and applying theories about what actually motivates people was gaining popularity in both the academic and corporate worlds. While teaching university students about values in terms of motivation and persuasion and getting started in our work supporting leaders in organizations, authors such as Piaget, Maslow, Rokeach, and Kohlberg were creating a new level of awareness of values, that was becoming accessible to consultants and educators. So when we were, in the mid-1990s, associated with the Center for Creative Leadership and working with European leaders from our base in Brussels, Belgium, we jumped at the opportunity to begin working with Brian Hall and Benjamin Tonna. We found an immediate compatibility between our ideas and theirs and quickly established an enjoyable and informative camaraderie with them both. Their groundbreaking work drew on those earlier authors and offered a synthesis that was new.

Brian, an Anglican priest, and Benny, a Catholic priest, were both deeply rooted in the liberal and socially progressive religious community of the 1960s and fervently believed in making a difference in the lives of people. We owe a very great debt to Brian Hall and Benjamin Tonna for their pioneering work and their willingness to share their insights and deep experience, and for the great influence their work has had on our own. While their theory is rigorous, and well-founded in a long tradition leading to very useful thinking about the nature and dynamics of values, we came to see that their work also reflected a centuries-old bias we believe to be deeply ingrained in the Western mind, that "higher is better." It is a tacit assumption that some value sets are inherently more advanced and, therefore, more desirable than others — an idea that we will discuss further in Part II, and indeed throughout this book — with which we found ourselves increasingly at odds, and increasingly hard-put to defend against the thoughtful and challenging questions many of our students and clients were asking. As we progressed with our own work and understanding of values theory and practice, we began to realize that our orientation had gradually shifted to reflect a new set of assumptions. Fundamentally, our assumption is that all values, and values perspectives, have merit and should be understood in the differing contexts in which people live and work, rather than viewed as mileposts on the way to a prescribed set of values that we must strive for or somehow be considered less worthy, or worse, be considered psychologically regressive or even potentially pathological. We state this strongly because as far as we are aware, this view is different in essence from the values stage development theories which have been historically presented and continue to characterize how human values are described.

In the course of our consulting and coaching experience over decades with corporate, educational, governmental, and other not-for-profit organizations, we have used a large number of different kinds of assessments. For example, the familiar MBTI (Myers-Briggs Type Indicator), the FIRO-B (Fundamental Individual Relations Orientation-Behavior); less familiar to some may be the KAI (Kirton Adaption-Innovation inventory), SYMLOG (SYstem for the Multiple Level Observation of Groups); and more recently introduced instruments like the Gallup Q-12 (a group assessment for high performance), and the Gallup SF34 (an individual strengths identification instrument). All of them are rigorously researched, constructed and validated, which means they provide reliable sources for descriptions of fundamental human personality and cognitive preferences. We began to recognize links between values and the concepts these instruments measure. We realized a new generation of values theory and assessment needed to be developed that would take these and other instruments like them into account.

We also needed to simplify values theory and values assessment to make it accessible to anyone living and working in any context or situation. We wanted to recognize and incorporate the wisdom and usefulness of what had gone before, yet avoid what we saw as the pitfalls. Our friends and associates had been asking us to do this work for some time, but we had resisted. Finally, we found ourselves in the position of being able to and needing to respond to their requests. So we took a deep breath, and began the work. The summary of that work is in this book.

In order to build our argument, and present a solution to the two propositions above—how to make values both consciously accessible and useful—we will have to do several things. First, before we dive into that tradition of values thinking, we will explain some of the basic characteristics and dynamics of values. That will set the stage for some digging into the historical contributions that have formed the grounding for much of how we think about values presently. That review, Part II of this book, is somewhat lengthy, but necessary to understand from where we come, and why the Values Perspective takes the shape it has. Then we can begin to build a solid theoretical foundation that will support our and others' insights and observations based on experience of working with individuals and groups, mostly in organizational settings, from a wide span of contexts and situations.

In Part III, we will suggest a set of characteristics that describe values and the way they work. We will also suggest a general framework that enables us to understand the dynamics of values so that they become both understandable to us and manageable. Since there are so many values, this is a necessary and powerful part of figuring out what to do in regard to values in our lives. The discussion of that framework can be summarized in the Values Perspective model.

The framework for working with values allows for four things: 1) surveying individual value choices 2) comparing those choices to the framework, or model, in order for an individual to understand the practical implications of their value choices; if desired 3) compare those choices to the choices of others in a given setting, and 4) interpret the resulting comparison in a way that allows an individual or group to make conscious decisions based on their goals and desires, given their views and their reach. These are the issues that are most often addressed when people think about, or talk about values development.

Values and development are fundamentally linked and most of our own work with executives and organizations, as well as with students, is about their own development. We have found, and we hold to this quite strictly, that before we can launch into discussions about development, where someone or some group is going, it is imperative to know where one is. The ordering of those two, assessment, then development, is critical. Otherwise, we know that people have a difficult time separating who they are from who they want or need to be. Those two may be the same, but most often they are different. And when they are, then that is where the interpretation and work actually begins. And this will be the main thrust of Part IV in our discussion.

As a way of helping people understand and interpret their priorities, it is useful to identify how values hold together in the natural world of being human. Values are not isolated; rather they connect to each other in supporting or leading ways to form clusters and tracks. The identification of these sorts of structures is extremely helpful for people as aids to interpreting their values. And since values drive behavior, it is important to discuss the relationship between values and behavior. In practice, the same value may be defined differently by a different person or group, and different behavioral choices are likely to be the result. Thus, clearly defining one's values, and what behaviors one expects of oneself and others has to be part of any values dialogue.

Finally, Part V is directed at the values practitioner, whether that is a single individual interested in her or his self-understanding, or a manager, consultant, or coach who may be using the Values Perspective model and perhaps survey on behalf of another person, group, or entire organization. Ours is a "strengths based" approach, meaning that our assumption is that a person's values are right for him, or for her. It is important to recognize that, while we may be able to apply some of all or our values with ease and skill, in which case, our values are indeed our strengths, it is also likely that we have become habitual about our behaviors, and may not have fully developed the potential that a given value represents. The practitioner, from a Values Perspective approach, is not prescriptive about the values a person holds, or might hold, but acts more as a facilitator in providing questions and observations regarding how values and their associated behaviors might be further developed.

Part I: Introducing Values

What is most important? The answer is, "It depends." It depends on our greatest aspirations. It depends on what is on the shopping list. It depends on what we want to give our energy to, and what energizes us in return. It depends on what life demands of us, and it depends on what beliefs we hold. What is most important is what we attribute value to for a lifetime and in any given moment. It might be making sure that somehow, we can satisfy the most basic needs for protection and shelter for our family each day. It might be finding the next big idea that will make our company a standout success, or discover the best way to connect an interested buyer with our product. It might be always telling the truth. It might be making choices that preserve our independence in every situation. It might be creating beauty in every action we take. It might be any or all of those things combined.

"Value" and "values" are words we hear often. Value can have an economic meaning, that is, the price we are willing to pay for something we need or want. If we value it, we will buy. If we do not, we will not. One way or the other, the choice can be influenced by many factors. For example, a buying decision can arise from the need to protect an investment, like making an improvement to a house that is calculated to result in greater economic return. It could be because something awakens nostalgia in connection with a remembered object or place or person we want to feel close to. It may be because we have decided to make some change in our lives. It may be because we wish to give a gift, or reward someone else. Or, it simply may be that it does not answer to the priorities we have set for spending, and we pass it by. How are our choices related to our values?

Many times these choices are made without conscious reflection, or even awareness of the trigger that impelled us to make a certain choice. Even a rational decision can tap into our oldest memories and experiences, the things we are taught from childhood to see as right and wrong, better and worse, important and less important. Some are so deep we have lost conscious track of them. Our choices are also influenced by our immersion in cultural habits and traditions, very often so ingrained that they are invisible to us, and may have been likewise invisible to our parents and their parents before them. An immigrant to a new country is likely to experience a period of values adjustment, and even anxiety, feeling compelled to preserve what is familiar from his or her previous home, while learning what the values that may have drawn him or her to a new country really look like in terms of what people actually say and do, and how they expect others to behave. Anyone beginning a new job may experience something similar. How do our values condition our experience of the world?

We often hear values expressed in the public arena. We may be exhorted to approve, vote, donate or advocate based on a direct appeal to our citizenship values, our employee values, human values, or our religious values. Such messages will either trigger a positive response such as agreement, approval, or a feeling of fellowship or belonging, which draws us toward the message or its author; or a negative one, such as disagreement, or indignation. We may even feel revulsion toward the people endorsing the message: "They're wrong, those aren't *my* values." Or, "That's not how I define it!" Through language and behavior, we find ourselves drawn toward people who seem to share our sense of what is important. Similarly, we sense difference and may even feel repelled by individuals or institutions whose values we do not share. This dynamic of attraction and repulsion is going on all the time, operating like a software program that runs in the background, driving the operations of more visible 'apps.' Emotion, memory, belief and culture are all filters, sometimes unconscious, that make some decisions more complicated. Why are some people's values so different from other people's values?

Values are complex, and are driven by a myriad of human characteristics and conditions. We have just raised some of the fundamental questions about how values operate. There are many more. Are values strictly moral choices? Are they relative or absolute? What do they have to do with belief? Are some values better than others? Are there bad values? What values should we have? How many values are there? What *are* values? So how do we understand and work with values? The purpose of this book is to provide you with an understanding of human values that you can then engage like an engine for personal growth and professional development.

We know that values are basic to human motivation and we all make choices every day about what we are going to do with our time and energy based on the values we hold. Shared values attract us to the individuals and groups we see eye-to-eye with and we make friendships and join groups of people accordingly. Value conflicts cause us to avoid or feel critical of others and those conflicts may tend to be strongly felt. How we value people and things causes us to act in one way or another.

Here is a simple definition for a value: *A value is a human quality to which we attribute importance, which we express by means of what we think, say and do, and recognize in what others say and do*. In light of all the questions above, the definition may seem over-simplified. Indeed, we never hold just a single value. Not only that, the values we do hold interact, and do so according to a number of principles we will explain as we go along. However, the simple definition is quite deliberate, and describes the basics of human values. We value what we hold to be important, for any of a universe of possible reasons. The values we hold drive the choices we make. These choices result in what we say (to ourselves and others) and in the actions we take. We interpret the values of others through the words they use, and the behaviors we observe.

Some of the confusion about values arises from the ways in which, through the last century, values have been described in terms analogous to the trajectory of human physical, emotional, and moral development. The most recent human value models group values into successive stages or worldviews that are based on earlier models describing how we develop from childhood to adulthood. There are advantages to using these stages as a way to group certain clusters of values, as we will demonstrate, but the greatest single disadvantage and inaccuracy is that physical and emotional development generally follow a directional, age-linked pathway from lesser to greater: from less ability, in childhood, to more ability as adults; from immature self-centeredness to mature self-control and awareness. In reality, once we reach physical and emotional maturity, growth and development cease to be linear and perhaps, in the views of some developmental theorists, never truly were linear at all. Applying child-to-adult development models to values requires that we see values as hierarchically ordered and implies that some clusters of values, because they are more advanced, are more desirable than others. Our work questions that assumption. We will discuss how values have been defined historically in Part II.

In short, we have found that returning to basics to look closely at what values are and are not, gives us a simpler and more effective way of understanding and working with values, and freeing that understanding from a historical bias that would lead us to assume that some values are better than others. Our main intention is to articulate, in the simplest possible terms, the complexities of how values operate. This makes it easier to recognize what values we hold, whether these values have been chosen for reasons we can state, or whether some of our values are received from upbringing and cultural norms (whether, for example, the culture be ethnic/linguistic or that of a group, team or organization in which we operate). We will raise questions that enable individual value recognition and discernment, and that give us ways to recognize—and to value—the values of other people.

Values are Energy

A useful way we have found to work with values is to think of them as a kind of energy. The things that are important to us we experience energetically. The energy can be mental, physical, emotional, or spiritual. As little as hearing or reading a single word can carry a substantial energetic charge, be it positive ("I like that!") or negative ("That is bad!" "How can they think that!") Positive values energy—feeling that I share the same value or values—moves me toward a person or situation. Negative values energy—feeling that someone does not share the same values or our values are in conflict—is likely to leave me uninterested or even drive me away. The values we hold act as motivators, which impel our decisions to place energy in a particular direction. If I value community, I will tend to look for opportunities to participate in, promote, or co-create whatever I define as community. Directing my attention in such a way will be energizing to me. In fact, if the value is important enough, it may seem as if it has an energetic force of its own.

Energy implies action. At the same time, we are not necessarily talking about the kind of energy described by the force placed on a billiard ball, which then moves in a given physical line of force. Some values operate that way. For example, I may value honesty, and my honesty, if I do not equally value harmony, may hold an energetic force that can knock people over. And, people may also understand that they will always get the straight story from me, and not have to worry that they may not know what I am thinking. On the other hand, holding a particular value, like respect, does not always necessarily result in a corresponding behavior, or in a behavior that is recognizable to another person as what they think of as respect. I may simply lack sufficient skill to realize it. Nevertheless, if I value respect, I will try to act in accordance with how I define that value. I will put energy in the direction of realizing my value of respect, through the way I try to interact with people and the skills I may seek in order to interact more successfully, such that people feel respected, and offer me respect in return.

Still other values are representative of aspirations. For example, I may value collaboration, I think it is important, and I would *like* to be able to participate in a collaborative team effort. I am seeking the opportunity; perhaps, the teams I have sought to collaborate with in the past have lacked the skills. Perhaps I lack the skills, but I still know it is important to collaborate, and I like to talk about it with like-minded people. I may be seeking the skills for collaboration, and this excites me, gives me energy.

Values are Choices

Some think that values are part of an individual's unchanging core, the essence of who each one of us is. Indeed, there may be some 'hard-wiring' involved in each of our personal set of values, and we may hold certain values very deeply and for a lifetime. However, just as humans can and do change as a result of experience and learning, values, too, are fundamentally changeable. Here is the key: once our values become conscious, they can be changed. They are subject to individual choice. Understanding how values operate in your life to drive your dreams, decisions, and actions will help you to make more conscious value choices in your life and work.

We have said that many choices we make are impelled by factors of which we may be unaware. These factors, such as what we are taught as children, or the cultural frameworks we have been brought up in, contribute to creating values we may hold. Some we will be very aware of; others we may not be aware of as a driving force in our lives. Some values, such as those for example having to do with belonging to a group or recognition for our accomplishments, may have been in place so long that they operate below the level of consciousness, and we may not even realize they are working, and energizing—or de-energizing—to us. Being asked a simple question, for example, if a boss takes the time to ask "How do you want to be rewarded?" can bring a value like recognition into conscious focus. Not only that, but we may also find in this conscious focus the opportunity to reflect on what recognition means to us (A cash reward? My name announced in a group meeting? My boss taking my spouse and me out to lunch and telling my spouse how much I contribute to the team?). When a value comes into conscious focus through choice, or through being called into awareness by circumstances, it is equally important that we take the time to understand exactly what that value means to us.

New values may be presented to us by necessity. Adults usually do not consciously seek skills without a reason for doing so. At times, we find ourselves in a situation where something other than what we hold as important comes to the fore. I may not have had to think as much about safety as other parts of my job responsibilities until I am appointed a safety team leader. I quickly find myself having to learn about aspects of workplace safety I never knew, and may come to deeply value safety while spending conscious time and energy understanding it thoroughly. It is not that I never valued safety, and perhaps it was one of the values already in place from childhood instruction; that is, internalized but not finding much place in my conscious awareness. But now it has become more highly prioritized. In my new role, I may additionally decide I need to more highly prioritize the value of informing others because I now recognize that well-presented information contributes to workplace safety. Life situations change, and we may find ourselves with a new value, or find ourselves more highly prioritizing a value as we seek to learn the skills associated with it.

We may be inspired by a life event or by another person to give conscious value to something we never thought about before. Adolescence and early adulthood are times when what we value may go through significant changes. Think, for example of how students often begin to hold very expansive and idealistic values as their understanding of the world begins to expand through education or a widening sphere of experience. These may continue to be values that are held for the rest of one's life. Having a family calls for a re-prioritization of values, usually involving more attention to finances and to security, safety and health matters; matters that without a family we might not have valued as highly, or now value for very different reasons. Mid-life may present an opportunity to re-assess and to take on board different values than those that served previously. Entering the workforce, having a family, changing jobs, attaining to mid-life and empty-nesting or otherwise changing relationship status, and entering elderhood; all present natural life opportunities to take on different perspectives and to make different value choices.

At any of these times, we may find ourselves in situations in which factors come into play that may cause us to think and behave in ways that may not be in alignment with what we believe to be our values. We might feel anxious, or stressed, or somehow less comfortable than we have been accustomed to. These factors can be external or internal, conscious or unconscious, and we may find ourselves asking the question "Why am I doing this?" Such a question may lead to an examination of the values we hold and sometimes a conscious change in some of those values. Some people ask this question of themselves, as part of an internalized habit of healthy periodic introspection. But, often life events that seem to be thrust upon us spur this introspection. At such times, what we value is likely to change.

Of course, there is no natural law that says values *must* be changed, or that one set of values is more or less correct than another. If we know some basics about how values operate and what our own values are, we can make the conscious choice to re-prioritize our values or to take on board different ones should we wish to do so. They are our values: it's up to us.

Values are Priorities

A value is a human quality to which we attribute importance. It follows that not all values can be equally important. We may hold any of perhaps thousands of possible human values, to some degree or another, but we tend to focus our energy through relatively few values at any given time in life. The values we prioritize most highly are the ones that will most energetically drive our thoughts and actions, and are those that others will most likely discern in our words and behaviors. These values are like cardinal points on a compass and we use them to keep ourselves oriented. To the degree we are conscious of them, we will tend to use these values as watchwords that guide our lives.

Our highest-priority values are in operation all the time, to some degree. We think of values as packets of energy; the highest-priority values evoke the most energy, so that we feel them, and others feel this energy as well. Further, if my highest-priority value is integrity, it is likely that this value will influence the other high-priority values I hold. For example, if I also highly value problem-solving, it is likely that the way I go about solving a problem will strongly reflect my value of integrity. I may be unlikely to cut corners, or to sacrifice what my definition of integrity leads me to view as important. It is likely too, that others will regard me as having integrity, to the degree I am capable of actualizing this value through consistency in my words and actions.

The order of our values priority is also dynamic. Even in the course of an ordinary day, certain values may be called to the fore, and others recede, as different events and challenges unfold. It is also possible that our set of highest-priority values, the ones that concern us more or less daily, may require us to trade off one value for another in a given situation, whereby the required value becomes more highly prioritized, according to the needs of the situation. For example, my value of financial success comes to the fore in a business negotiation. An hour later I may be operating through my value of empathy when required to make a difficult decision regarding a sensitive employee issue, where financial success may take second, or third, place. These will be values that are already highly prioritized for me. If I am a different person, I may be calling on the values of honesty and fairness in the same situations.

One of the mechanisms for values development is that I may be called upon to operationalize a value that is not a high priority value for me. As in the example above, a person whose highest-priority values are integrity and problem-solving may for example be called upon to give priority to the value of strategy in order to better support business development. As I learn about strategy and it takes a greater precedence among my values, I will still value integrity, and this value will continue to influence how I think, what I say, and what I do, and my capacity as a strategist will be characterized by my value of integrity. Too, I will likely still value problem solving, and this too will influence how I value strategy.

It is also possible that a high-priority value may cede precedence to a new value. As a new parent, I may recognize a need to give self-sacrifice higher priority over achievement. This may mean I will need to find new ways to think about, define and satisfy my value of achievement. If I have not previously held self-sacrifice as a high-priority in my life, I will need to learn new ways of thinking and behaving through the lens of this value, in order to accomplish what I now see as most important.

Values and Development

Our primary objective in doing this work is to provide you with a set of tools with which to further your own, and perhaps your group or organization's effectiveness and best meet personal and professional objectives. We have already said that this does not imply that as a result of working with your values you will or should change some or any of them. Nor does this imply that some values are better or more important than others. It is important to recognize that the eventual intent of this book is to help you further your own development, based on your particular potential, personality, and situation. It is our assumption that you are not 'broken,' and the purpose of this work is not to 'fix' you. This is our way of saying that we respect each person's and each group's values as those which are important for them at that time. The sole aim here is an informed conversation that benefits the development of the individual and, by extension, the collective in which he or she may play a part.

What we mean by 'development' in regard to values is threefold. First, that you are able to better recognize and understand your values and how they operate, which will then allow you to make better choices about how you apply and live your values. Second, that you are able to better recognize and understand how the values of others operate. This involves discerning differences in how you and others view the world, because, as we will describe in Part III of this book, we not only have differences in values, but in the values-worldview—we call this a perspective—that organizes our general view on the world. This can differ from person to person and from institution to institution and from culture to culture. A difference in perspective requires understanding the point of view of those holding a different perspective in order to meaningfully communicate, influence and successfully coexist. Third, values can change, according to the principles we've just discussed: energy, choice and priority. It is very important to understand that when such changes occur, they may engage us in bringing to the fore values we have not previously considered important. We may not have even considered them worthy; in short, we have not *valued* them. Conscious engagement in the change process will result in better results, personally and professionally.

Values development begins with the individual. It applies by extension to groups, along similar principles. We will talk more about the process of values alignment within groups, in Part IV. It is also important to understand that an individual must understand her or his own values in order for group values development to occur.

Our intention is that you will gain solid insights about how your interactions with others may be understood and improved. We assume that everyone, ourselves included, can find opportunities to expand the skills and behaviors we need to realize values we already hold as important. And, we can expand our values 'reach' into new areas that depend on values that are new to us.

Making Values Conscious

We have noted that we may not be conscious of many of our values, and that making values conscious allows us to understand how we can best make use of our values, and even decide to change them. We have also observed that most people are not able to easily identify very many of their own values. Still less, define them and explain how those values operate in their lives. When we ask people for their values, they may commonly be able to name three or four, but have usually not reflected much on more than one or two, and have not thought about how they might interact to produce thoughts and actions.

Life conditions can bring values to the fore, as when my value of duty may be activated by a family or community emergency, and all of my immediate energy goes into participation. When asked, I might be able to name this value. When asked further, what it has meant in my life, I will likely be able to say when I first became aware of it, perhaps what family or educational or experiential conditions or influences called it forth.

We find that asking questions is the most reliable way of surfacing values into conscious view. The simplest question is, "What is most important to you?" The next question, of course, is "Why?" Then, "How does it show up in your life?" "Where did it come from?" From this point, any number of questions may be asked that will stimulate reflection and aid in the discernment of our values and what they mean to us.

When working with values, the first steps are to identify what values are in operation. This can be done through simple reflection, answering questions, or by means of a survey. Next, it is important to define a value, in other words, understand and clearly articulate what that value means in one's experience and daily life. For example, one person may define playfulness as a childlike quality that leads them to see humor in ordinary things. They love to make lighthearted fun of the people and situations around them, and they love making people laugh. Another person may define playfulness as a physical activity, involving games or perhaps practical jokes, anything that gets them and other people moving, and maybe they love to tickle and roughhouse like kids. We all define our values somewhat differently, given that our experience, psychological and cognitive preferences and cultural frame of reference are unique and individual. When people compare their definitions of the same value, the differences can be startling. Next, it is important to validate a value. How does it show up in my life? Do other people see it in me? Am I really living up to it? Or, perhaps, is another value really more important? Is there anything I would do to live this value more fully?

People define values differently. We also prioritize them differently, and recognizing this priority is an important part of values discernment. An interesting exercise is to present a small set of common values and ask a person to rank order them according to importance. Why is one value more important than another? In what situations might a lower-ranked value be placed more highly? When people share their rank-ordering of values with others in small groups, the results, like comparing definitions, can be surprising. This is a simple tool that leads to deeper dialogue, and we have often seen two people, whom we have asked to carry out this exercise because their values differences are obvious and perhaps, openly acknowledged, come to mutual understanding that becomes a basis for resolving conflict.

Making values conscious and giving attention to how we define and prioritize our values leads to greater awareness of self and of others, which in turn allows for conscious decision-making that allows us to live our values more fully. The steps above lead to self-reflection and are the basis for understanding oneself better, and making some choices about life and work. These steps can be used by an individual, among friends or family, or in a coaching or counseling relationship.

Surveying Values

The most effective way of making values and value priorities conscious is through a questionnaire or survey. This is useful for individuals, who are able to choose and prioritize from a values list. It is especially useful in groups, when individual results may be aggregated to present a 'snapshot' of the values energy averaged across a group. To the degree that values are dynamic and changeable, a survey can be assumed to discern values that are current priorities. A group or individual going through significant change would present at least a slightly, and perhaps greatly, different values "field" if sampled through an extended period of time.

In a survey process, the individual is presented with a robust list of values and their definitions. The definition of each value should be clear, unambiguous, as concise as possible and ideally, should be presented in the mother-tongue or language most used by the person taking a values survey. People tend to define, interpret and behavioralize the same value differently, according to what we term their perspective, which is essentially a basic worldview. An effective survey allows room for such interpretation. An accompanying report, individual coaching or counseling, or a group values alignment process should provide means for the person who has taken a survey to refine their personal definition and validate its meaning in their life.

The minimum number of values presented must be sufficient to reflect a spectrum of human experience and concerns, and to allow consideration of why one value might be more important, more fundamental, or more broadly applicable than another, in that person's judgment. By its nature, a survey presents a vehicle for conscious choice among values, as the person taking the survey is presented with value choices to affirm as important, or discard as less important based on deliberation as values are presented. In this way, the process of surveying itself should be an exercise in conscious values discernment. People taking the Values Perspective Survey very often remark on how much it made them think about their priorities, and how insightful it was to do so.

We have found that most values theories and accompanying surveys are built on the assumption that there are some values that are somehow better or higher in terms of moral development than others. This is a very important point because if the structure of a survey implies that some values should be understood as more desirable than others, people often begin to put aside their own priorities, and begin to select what they believe may be considered desirable by some external standard of judgment. This effectively puts a stop to genuine development and can do damage to the person and to any group process concerning values. We will come back to this point several times throughout this book.

The Values Perspective Survey does not provide any indication or inference as to what any person's values should be. It is not prescriptive in any way. The purpose of any values measure should first of all, be to help simplify the process of working with values. And although assessments and measures are useful, the processes of values identification and alignment are not dependent on instruments or measures.

Aligning Values

Group and organization effectiveness is enhanced by holding shared values that are accepted and well understood by constituents. A deep values alignment involves laying on the table the set of values that is actually in operation within a group, and then asking the question, "What should the values for the entire group be, given its mission, or objectives?" The discussion that follows can be time consuming, and contentious. True values alignment is a relative rarity because it is not so easy. An attempt at values alignment can be seriously counter-productive when underlying dynamics are dysfunctional and the real set of values in operation are hidden or contrary to stated values. A misguided or uninformed attempt to align values in such circumstances can be perceived as cynical at best and deepen divisions and value differences that are already present and real.

When values are placed on the table, people get energized—positively or negatively—by what is most important to them, how they define it and what behaviors they will expect to see in order to know someone is living the value according to how they see it. A values alignment process must provide structures to keep discussions respectful, productive and safe for the participants. However time consuming or difficult it may be, creating the opportunity for this kind of dialogue is the only way to arrive at a shared set of values, not just a poster on the wall or a wallet card with words on it.

When working to align values within a group (which we will discuss at greater length in Part V), coming to mutual understanding, and eventual agreement, on a set of values follows basically the same set of steps outlined above. First, identify what values are in operation. In group settings, a survey is a highly effective means for doing so, and values selected by participating individuals can be aggregated to give an anonymous group values profile. Anonymity is vital for individuals to feel safety in a values alignment process. Value choices may be shared at will, but coming to agreement on a set of values in a group does not depend on knowing what each member individually values. It is a matter of coming to agreement on what a group decides to prioritize given their mutual goals. Aggregated survey results will indicate where the values energy, and thus potential, lies within a group. In this book, we will provide sufficient theory to help a practitioner understand value dynamics such that a group may be facilitated to maximize potential and to understand how to get from an operating values set to a desired values set.

Existing values can be amplified and desired values can be added. Which among the values that are presently energized serve our identity and our goals as a group? Do we see in our aggregate sample values that represent potential energy, which some among us hold and as a group we would like to reprioritize? In other words, what values represent strengths we can access through diversity? What values may be missing, that we need to consciously adopt? Have we left anything out that is vital?

The second step is to define values the group wishes to amplify, and values the group wishes to activate. This stage requires that a value is carefully defined, so that everyone knows what it means. This requires dialogue, and may lead to certain values being recognized as more important, higher-priority than others; some may be recognized as supportive of other values and thus necessary to reach, a mechanism that will be further discussed in Part IV.

The third step is to discuss and come to mutual agreements about what constitutes a selected value in action 'on the ground,' that is, what behaviors reflect the value, and what behaviors do not. Based on these understandings, agreements can be made with regard to behavioral expectations, and all participants will have a shared picture of what is most important, why, and what to do about it. Above all, it should be made explicitly clear that alignment with a group's agreed-upon set of values does not mean individuals must or should change or give up personal values.

The final step is to periodically revisit those values with their definitions, and the group's agreements and understandings about them to see if the list needs refining, perhaps expanding, maybe shortening, because living with the awareness of those values will always result in further insights into them, and the interconnections between them. These insights will likely lead to new agreements and revised action plans.

The Ethics of Working with Values

Everyone is entitled to hold his or her set of personal values. Human emotional maturity means making trade-offs when a situation demands it. We are all works in progress with regard to our attitudes, emotions, and our development of the skills needed to successfully and harmoniously navigate life in a world filled with people who hold differing values, for whatever good and worthy reasons and circumstances. Knowing more about how values operate gives important insights into our own "operating manual." It also gives vital insights into how others may value, and what is important to them. With this understanding, we can choose how to approach people and situations with sensitivity and effectiveness. We can learn what questions to ask, and how to offer information about ourselves and our concerns in a way that can be understood and respected.

Ethics refers to a general, social code or system of decisions and behavior that identify what is accepted as morally correct or at least acceptable. There is in our opinion an ethics of working with values. When we work with values, a "prime directive" is safety for any individual whether in a one-on-one coaching or counseling setting, in a team, or in the context of a small or large organization or institution. Safety means, primarily, confidentiality. No one should be compelled to share what is personal to him or her. When using survey results, individual values profiles should always remain confidential, meaning that an individual may choose to share some or all of his or her results, by his or her own wish or by un-coerced agreement, but should under no circumstances be compelled to do so. Any consultant, internal or external to any organization, should abide by a standard code of professional ethics in conducting values work that includes confidentiality and to clearly state this as a standard of conduct.

We know of instances when information gained from a values survey was used to recommend firing. We consider this to be gravely unethical. An ethical approach to working with values recognizes and manages the legitimate authority of an institution, organization, manager, or leader to prescribe a normative set of values and behaviors to those people associated with them, balanced against the interests and wellbeing of the individual within that context. As any consultant knows, this can be a delicate balance, and the ethics of consulting practice generally is far beyond the scope of this book. However, with this in mind, we suggest some basics regarding working with values assessment and development.

No one's personal values are inherently any better or superior to another's values. We know of no evidence that suggests that holding a certain set of values means an individual is more or less capable of effectiveness on the job. Further, it cannot be assumed that a selection of values automatically results in associated behaviors, either negative or positive. It is important to use this work for discovery, and dialogue, and to refrain from judgment. A values selection may be helpful in forming hypotheses, which then must be tested and validated, or invalidated.

This work should never be used for either performance measurement or selection purposes, meaning that it should never be used to disqualify a job candidate. This is not a question of match. Values are changeable, complex and dynamic; therefore, by themselves, an inadequate measure for determining fit. However, values may be used as a beginning point of discussion and exploration, for example between a manager and subordinate in appreciative inquiry. Using a values lens is also an excellent way for a candidate to get to know a prospective organization and to guide questions about the organization's values. Prospective employers are generally very impressed with a candidate who grasps the organization's DNA and can articulate it, ask meaningful questions, and offer relevant experience and qualifications. Understanding the values I may bring to a situation, and the values of the situation, position or company I am considering contributing my energy to, is a mutual benefit. If I understand my own values, and the basics of how values operate, I can ask highly informed questions about an organization that will allow me to determine whether my value set will align or not.[1] Likewise, a recruiter may ask, "What's important to you? What do you want from this position? How do this company's values connect with your own?" We will present an example in Part IV of how a multi-national organization constructively envisions a very wide values "reach" among its employee mix.

Finally, any values theory or survey that presumes to tell you who you are, that is, attempts to identify personality or cognitive traits from your values selection, is reaching too far, and such claims cannot be substantiated. That is why, in our values work, we find questions more important than answers. The theory, the survey, and the methods described in this book are intended to provide the starting point for dialogue—with oneself and with others—in order to arrive at outcomes of understanding, relationship building, constructive influence, and of development.

---

1 See Cheryl De Ciantis and Kenton Hyatt, *Looking for Work with Values* (2009), accessed July 2, 2013, http://www.kairios.com.

Part II:
Historical Roots and Influences

We are still influenced by the thinking of the Greek philosophers with regard to both values and development. However, while our work is concerned with development, the Greeks were concerned with one central question: how should we live? [2] Thus, the origin of values lies in ethics, which asks questions about how we know and act upon the difference between what is good and what is bad in human life.

For the most part, Greek philosophers and the field of philosophy in general have contributed most to the ethical aspects of our understanding of values. Psychology has had somewhat more to say about the structure and nature of values themselves. Ethics is a branch of philosophy, and addresses, more than just the issue of what is good or bad behavior, how we can know the difference and even extends to the question of whether the basic nature of humans is good or evil. Values are at the heart of ethics, and can account, in part, for the ethical or unethical nature of decisions and behaviors of the kind we hear every day in the news. Ethics couples values and cultural morality, and provides a system of what should be done given basic principles and assumptions. Ethics are prescriptive, whereas values, in and of themselves, are not, but they are motivational.

2 Martha Nussbaum, *The Fragility of Goodness* (New York: Cambridge University Press, 1986). See Chapter 1.

The Greeks: Values as Making Choices

The English word "value" has no single corresponding term in Greek. Related words refer to that which is "good" or "fine," or to the concept of intrinsic goodness. Also, worthiness, choice worthiness, and terms that involve estimating, esteeming, and choosing.[3] Thus, from the Greeks we have the concept of values as choices. From the early writings of Plato, we also receive the idea that there are some values that are overarching. They are seen to be more important than, and are of necessity supported by, subordinate values. For example *integrity*, or acting according to what one declares one believes, is such a governing value.[4]

The idea that values operate in rankings or priorities when compared with other values is an important one, leading us to two conclusions. First, that values link together in meaningful ways and second that this linking occurs in a manner that gives some values priority over others. This turns out to be of particular and powerful importance, as we will see that, for later writers, this implies that one value can be considered to be of a "higher level" than another. We'll examine the problems that arise from this second notion more fully a little later.

Socrates, in the writings of Plato, struggles with two problems. The first is defining what a value actually is. Plato's *Laches* examines the nature of courage. The examination occurs in the form of a dialogue between two generals, both of whom are known to be courageous. However, neither can define it. [5] Socrates finally concludes that values resist definition, are not instinctual or innate and therefore must be a gift from the gods, and require learning to understand. But, the problem remains of how to teach values given that they resist definition. Further, virtues may be taught but this does not mean that students will always become good people as a result.

Aristotle lays the groundwork for establishing that values are subject to the rational mind, making rationality an overarching value. In the *Nicomachean Ethics*, Aristotle names several of the concepts we think of as values, for example, courage, temperance, magnanimity, patience, truthfulness, and modesty. He defines "goodness" as "living well and doing well."[6] It is important to understand that Aristotle and the Greeks

---

3 Ibid., 7.

4 Plato, *Meno,* trans. Benjamin Jowett (Whitefish, MT: Kessinger Publishing, 2004).

5 Plato, *Laches or Courage*, trans. Benjamin Jowett, accessed July 7, 2010, http://philosophy.eserver.org/plato/laches.txt.

6 Nussbaum, 6.

do not understand values as abstract moral standards, but as essentially active behavior. Put simply, being good is inseparable from doing well. Truthfulness is manifested through behaviors such as self-expression; the opposite of truthfulness is manifested through boastfulness or withholding truth. And here, two more assumptions about values are revealed, assumptions which are very much in operation today. The first is that values are fundamentally and inextricably linked to behavior. The second is that there is a fundamental importance in the correspondence between what is spoken, and what is done. Put simply, "walking the talk" is a very old idea, one that has not lost its importance for us.

While for Socrates the gods were the source of values and good, for Aristotle human rationality begins to be the means to discover and communicate about values. Excellence derives from human choices and actions. And, ethics has a great deal to do with whether and how we perceive others acting out of values similar to our own. In fact, we tend to refuse to give credibility to those who do not. Holding differing values can then be expected to lead to conflict between individuals or groups. At the same time, for the Greeks, not all behaviors are governed by rationality. The contingencies of luck, or fate, or strong passions might force people to make value choices that conflict with their desires for good and bring them into conflict with the community.[7]

Although the Greeks did not solve some of the problems they pondered, like defining what a value is, they did provide us with the groundwork of assumptions about values that govern our understanding of them, even today. We owe to the Greeks the concept of values and their relation to choices that result in positive outcomes in human life, and that values interact in different ways. And ethics was established as a way to describe and discuss the relationship between values and behavior.

Modern Philosophical Influences: Values as Moral Imperatives

Two important modern philosophers, Emanuel Kant and John Stuart Mill, need to be mentioned when discussing values because, like the Greeks before them, they have had a lasting influence on our current understanding and application of values. Like the ancient Greeks, Kant relies on rationality as the primary method by which values are both

7 Ibid., 7.

selected and applied, and in this, he also assumes the idea of choice, that values can be selected. But he extended this assumption to address the questions of what values should be selected and why they are chosen. His "categorical imperative" is one of the most cited principles for the establishment of policy in terms of ethics and morality. Simply, it says that we can be sure that a given decision is ethical if it can be universally applied. It follows then that the most moral values are always those that are most universally applicable. Kant named rational integrity alone, among all other values, as the overarching governing principle for making judgments that we may then hold as rigorously correct.[8]

John Stuart Mill is considered to be the best representative of what is called the philosophy of Utilitarianism (although Jeremy Bentham, another utilitarian philosopher who preceded Mill also described similar views). Two Utilitarian concepts Mill articulated contribute to our current understanding of working with values. The principle of greatest happiness states that the most moral actions are those that result in the greatest amount of happiness for the greatest number of people. The principle of greatest harm states that we are free to do what we want, as long as our actions do not harm other people. Both principles place primary moral and ethical emphasis on the effect a decision or action has on the general group or society.[9] Both Kant and Mill are concerned with what is ethical, which includes both what is important (values) and what is moral (what actions or behaviors *should* support the values).

Our heritage from Kant is highly significant because it provides us with the roots of some of the major assumptions and principles that govern much of values theory: some actions are moral, others are immoral, and moral value must be considered to be greater.[10] Perhaps, most useful for this discussion is the recognition that these principles tie individual values to both behavior and its effects or impacts on others. The assumption behind these principles is that what we do is not neutral, but is attached to values; therefore, ethical guidelines regarding behavior are justifiable.

Martha Nussbaum, Professor of Law and Ethics at the University of Chicago, points out that the moral or value imperatives articulated by Kant and the Utilitarians differ greatly from the Greeks in that "no matter what happens in the world, the moral value of the good will remains

---

8 Immanuel Kant, *Groundwork of the Metaphysics of Morals*, (New York: Cambridge University Press, 1998).

9 John Stuart Mill, *Utilitarianism, ed.* George Sher, (Indianapolis, IN: Hackett Publishing Inc., 2001).

10 Nussbaum, 4.

unaffected."[11] The positive benefits of the logical rigor of the Kantian view allow us to create firm moral standards to govern ourselves by. However, in this view, complex situational and emotional influences are devalued. The idea that our choices can be, and ought to be made without situational and emotional influence is well described. And this idea has been, and still is a point of difficulty for society, as we will discover later in this discussion.

Because Kant and Mill put the idea forward that values are held and sustained by a group or society, we can now understand the emphasis and importance of Aristotle's view that "ethical theorizing proceeds by way of a reflective dialogue."[12] The Socratic dialogues show that when people are asked to say what they believe, their statements usually do not reflect the actual complexity of their beliefs and values.[13] That complexity is held within the context of the society or group. However, according to Aristotle, people arrive at a clearer understanding of their beliefs through reflective dialogue with others, and ultimately their agreements with others through this process will reveal the ethical truth. Nussbaum asserts that this is "a truth that is anthropocentric, not relativistic."[14] That is, the values that are held by society as a whole, or by a specific group, are arrived at by some sort of dialogue and a sort of tacit negotiation that occurs over time. So the saying, "Well, you've got your opinion, and I've got mine," is not the way values are actually established nor maintained.

We agree, and in the approach we are offering to you in this book, we emphasize the primacy of the individual in values assessment, followed by the development of consensus values and their priorities, and their respective, operational definitions. Most importantly, in this approach to values, a group must conduct a dialogue so that divergent and minority views may be heard, and these insights and perspectives incorporated into the values view articulated by the group. The approach is first on the individual's understanding of his or her values, then on his or her role in the group, and finally on the group's role of inclusion and self-alignment of all of its members, for its own optimal effectiveness.

---

11 Ibid., 4.

12 Ibid., 10.

13 "Plato shows us how Glaucon, an ordinary gentleman, discovers in himself, through conversation with Socrates, an intense love for the pure and stable activity of mathematical reasoning, a love that requires the denigration of much that he had previously valued." Ibid., 5.

14 Nussbaum, 11.

The approach we suggest does not leave the establishment of the ultimate standards of goodness or even acceptability to the whim of each person's desire or needs. However, it does recognize and respect the individual's values. Values *are* held individually, and they are also compared, confirmed, and many times negotiated by people in groups to create an understanding of what is not only accepted, but can result in a normative code of behaviors. Prior to values alignment, there is always a code, often tacit and unspoken, but nevertheless a code that is quite powerful, of "How we do things here." The code is highly prescriptive of our and others' behavior whether we are aware of it or not. This is an inter-subjective result of natural group alignment in which the values driving our behavior are so familiar to us that we have difficulty at times being able to clearly identify, much less articulate them. We will return to this issue later because one of our general objectives in writing this book is to help you become more aware of this connection, so as to then be able to exercise conscious choices in regard to what you do, and why you do it.

Psychological Influences: Values Linked to Development

There does not seem to be any argument about development itself. It is accepted as describing the process of change and growth leading toward full life participation in the human sphere of activity. In all cultures, and with all peoples, the idea of development is a fundamental part of maturing. Many developmental theories are primarily oriented toward describing human development up to adulthood, while some span the entirety of the human lifetime.

Without question, the majority of psychological development theory falls into a category called Stage Theory, which proposes that human development can be appropriately identified by significant periods in age, while the Continuous Development theorists argue that learning is a continual, incremental process[15]. But it is the stage theorists that values theory depends on, and quite heavily at that. For it has been the stage theorists who identified and categorized various values that emerge in human development.

The contrasting orientation, referred to as Incremental Theory, argues that development cannot be divided neatly into stages, that it is actually

15 Thomas Keenan and Subhadra Evans, "An Introduction to Child Development," 2d. ed. (Thousand Oaks, CA: Sage, 2009), 10.

much more subtle and gradual most of the time. Below, we will briefly identify the contributions, mostly from the stage theory perspective, which have most significantly influenced how we think about values. Authors will be presented in more or less historical order.

Erik Erikson

One of the most influential contributors to stage development theory is psychologist Erik Erikson, a student of Sigmund Freud. While Freud himself also proposed a series of developmental stages, Erikson's model includes not just childhood development as most stage theories do, but spans the entire lifetime. Erikson posits eight life stages describing psychological and social development, asserting that development is primarily driven by the needs of each stage. Erikson's concepts became the basis used by other authors to describe moral and values development. His stages are:

Stage 1	Stage 2	Stage 3	Stage 4	Stage 5	Stage 6	Stage 7	Stage 8
Trust vs. Mistrust	Autonomy vs. Shame/Doubt	Initiative vs. Guilt	Industry vs. Inferiority	Identity vs. Identity Confusion	Intimacy vs. Isolation	Generativity vs. Stagnation	Integrity vs. Despair
0-1 yr.	1-3 yrs.	3-5 yrs.	5-12 yrs.	Adolescent	Young	Mid-Adult	Late Adult

Fig. 1 — Summary of Erikson's Stages of Human Development

In Erikson's model, each stage can contain both positive and negative qualities. Fulfillment of the positive aspect of each stage is required for proper development in subsequent stages. However, if the negative quality of any given stage is internalized by an individual, its influence will color subsequent stage development, impairing development and resulting in a lack of fulfillment and satisfaction at the end of life.[16]

Jean Piaget

Jean Piaget is credited as being one of the first psychologists to focus solely on childhood development, applying a variation of Erikson's stage model as a basis for development theory in education. He identified three basic areas or components with which to describe development, which clearly took on the question of how a child matures in thinking to become a rational adult. Piaget's three areas of focus are schemas (the

16 Erik Erikson, *Childhood and Society*, 2nd ed., (New York: Norton, 1950), 222-246.

content of what is learned, i.e., knowledge), stages of development, and the processes by which a child changes or develops from one stage to another. Whereas Erikson assumes that the means for developmental "movement" through subsequent psychological stages is a natural result of physical age and maturation, Piaget attributed greater importance to social interaction as a contributing mechanism in the process of development. He suggested four stages of development: the Sensorimotor period for the first two years of life, the Preoperational period for ages 2-7, the Concrete period for ages 7-11, and the Formal Operational period for ages 11 to adult. [17] Each subsequent stage becomes more complex and represents a successively greater level of development than previous stages. The process by which children move from one stage to another is cyclical: Assimilation / Equilibration / A new Situation / Disequilibrium / Accommodation—which leads to Assimilation, and the potential for a new cycle. For Piaget, development was not a continuous process but was punctuated by situational events (i.e, discontinuous development events, for example, first steps or first words) that precipitated the development of the individual into a higher stage of development, although the stages themselves are universal to humans.[18]

Sensorimotor	Preoperational	Concrete Operational	Formal Operational
Reflexive; Coordination of sensory information and physical results 0-2 yrs.	Self-Oriented; Beginnings of symbolic representation through words and images 2-7 yrs.	Logical reasoning about concrete events; Able to classify ideas 7-11 yrs.	Reasoning is abstract; Thinking is more idealistic 11-15 yrs.

Fig. 2 — Summary of Piaget's Stages of Development

The legacy of Piaget is remarkable in values theory. Piaget is looked to as a foundational author in regard to human development. His child development model greatly influenced Kohlberg, and many authors following him. His recognition of a mechanism for development and its dependent assumption of discontinuous development is found throughout values stage models today.

17 Jean Piaget, *The Psychology of the Child*, (New York: Basic Books, 1972).

18 Saul McLeod, "Jean Piaget: Cognitive Theory," Simply Psychology, 2009, updated 2012, accessed July 8, 2012, http://www.simplypsychology.org/piaget.html.

Lawrence Kohlberg

Expanding and building on the social interaction mechanism described by Piaget, Lawrence Kohlberg developed a model of stages of moral development, which bears more directly on values theory than previous developmental stage descriptions. Like Piaget, Lawrence Kohlberg assumes that development is linked with age, and with social and cognitive dilemmas. As life progresses, we find ourselves facing increasingly difficult situations that contain moral dilemmas. Kohlberg clearly identifies the stage concept as a fundamental and integrated mechanism. The process of learning how to deal with those dilemmas is what propels us into the next stage of development. Kohlberg's model adds a layer of organization to previous stage models by positing three successive social/cognitive stages, each comprising two stages of moral development.[19] This is a summary of Kohlberg's stages of development.

Pre-Conventional		Conventional		Post-Conventional	
Stage 1	Stage 2	Stage 3	Stage 4	Stage 5	Stage 6
Guidance and Punishment	Individualism, Instrumentalism, Exchange	Good Boy/Girl	Law and Order	Social Contract	Principled Conscience

Fig. 3 — Summary of Kohlberg's Stages of Development

W. C. Crain, a developmental psychologist, observes that, "Kohlberg means that the stages are not just isolated responses but are *general* patterns of thought that will consistently show up across many different kinds of issues."[20] In defining the six stages of moral development, Kohlberg harkens back to Kant and Mill. The Pre-Conventional stages (1 and 2) are the successive stages of childhood and adolescence, leading to the Conventional stages (3 and 4). However, development through successive stages is not driven by age and physical maturation. Instead, Kohlberg states that the social norm for most adults is focused in the third or fourth stages, effectively culminating in the Conventional level. Moral development into the Post-Conventional stages (5 and 6) is based on an awareness of interdependency between persons that results in more sophisticated and

19 Lawrence Kohlberg, *The Psychology of Moral Development: The Nature and Validity of Moral Stages,* (San Francisco: Harper and Row, 1984).

20 Willaim C. Crain, *Theories of Development* (Upper Saddle River, NJ: Prentice Hall, 1985), 118-136.

collaborative relationships. This requires a much different sort of mindset than previous stages to comprehend and activate. Stage 6 is reserved for highly evolved people, and acts almost as a theoretical goal, but not one that is actually achieved by average people. Kohlberg maintained that morality is determined by one's relationship to convention, and he argued against a relativistic approach to morality. He combined moral development and conventionality into the continuum of development.[21]

Development through Kohlberg's stages is linear. One must achieve each stage before moving on to the next. His pedagogical approach is Socratic. He presents cases and examples of moral dilemmas to people who work though the example to come to an expanded level of consciousness, where the mindset of the next level begins to make sense to the person working with the example. Thus, a rational approach is relied upon in exploring situations and results in a new awareness. Kohlberg, like many others before and after, assumes that we may depend on rational cognition to develop morality. While Kohlberg does not specifically describe moral behaviors, he emphasizes choice at each stage.

Kohlberg's stage 6 is worth noting in particular because it contains qualities that act as requirements which few people ever seem to achieve. It comprises a sort of lineal hyper-extension of the developmental continuum. This is seen by many as exemplifying a particularly Western idea, related to the early Christian theological adaptation of the Greek idea of *telos*, or end-state, which envisions a definitive goal for human moral perfection. Indeed, examples cited for this stage include Mother Teresa, Martin Luther King, and Mahatma Gandhi. This reveals a decidedly difficult problem in terms of development. While the values contained in this stage are admirable, actually achieving this stage of development is reserved for very special, saint-like people, and poses a question regarding how we, as average people, are to achieve such a highly developed state. Is it actually possible to intentionally become so highly developed in an average lifetime? The underlying assumption in all of this is that each moral stage acts as an achievement. More than simply achieving a certain height at a given age, this achievement is based on rational choices that evolve with one's selection of values that correspond to higher levels.

However, Kohlberg does not account for situational influences that would require Post-Conventional /Social Contract reasoning at one

21 Elliot Turiel, *The Culture of Morality: Social Development, Context, and Conflict*, (Cambridge, England: Cambridge University Press, 2002), 101-102.

moment, and then Conventional /Law and Order reasoning at the next. Neither does he account for the power of the group in regard to holding and prescribing particular values and types of moral reasoning. His is a highly individualistic model. Nevertheless, Kohlberg remains one of the major influences in current values theory and models today.

Work with Kohlberg's theory continues. For example, psychologist James Rest and a group of his University of Minnesota colleagues (Darcia Narvaez, Muriel Bebeau, and Stephen Thoma, and others) have developed an assessment instrument called the Defining Issues test that is based on responses to five moral dilemmas. Individual responses are rated in terms of interests, norms and Kohlberg's Post-Conventional stages of development. This work has been called "Neo-Kohlbergian" by its authors and rests on the basic Kohlberg theory.[22]

David McClelland

David McClelland, following the 20th century Harvard psychologist, Henry Murray, identifies three basic needs that act as motivational forces driving behavior: achievement, power, and affiliation (abbreviated as N-Ach, N-Pow, and N-Aff respectively).[23] While McClelland used the term "needs" as connected to motivation, his needs function in the same way that others use the term "values," in the way they are used to both prioritize and motivate behavior. People are disposed to prioritize one of these three needs over the others. Thus, development depends on choice and situational influences, an idea we are familiar with from the Greeks. However, the research of Murray and McClelland demonstrates a verifiable link between psychological motivational factors and behavior. In organizational situations, people with high achievement needs were shown to maximize achievement (N-Ach) by means of risk-taking. People with high power needs (N-Pow) often find themselves as recipients of high levels of responsibility (equating to *social* power) and are highly motivated to influence and exert control over others (equating to *individual* power). People with high affiliation needs (N-Aff) tend to work well with

---

22 James Rest et al., "A Neo-Kohlbergian Approach: The DIT and Schema Theory," *Educational Psychology Review* 11, no. 4 (December 1999), 291-324.

23 Henry A. Murray, *Explorations in Personality,*(New York: Oxford University Press,1938), and David C. McClelland, *The Achieving Society* (Princeton: Van Nostrand, 1961). These three needs are independent of any developmental continuum, but McClelland's work in particular was highly influential on Maslow as discussed above, and on other stage model theorists as well as cultural model theorists.

interpersonal relationships, particularly in teams where collaboration and conflict management skills are important.[24]

Before McClelland, developmental stage theory, and particularly values theory had not been widely felt in organizational contexts. McClelland began to change the scope of the application of these theories, and his acceptance was in part, in our opinion, due to the simplification of his model and his application of the model to organizational contexts.

Abraham Maslow

One of the founders of the Humanistic Psychology movement, Abraham Maslow is well known for his Hierarchy of Needs. His orientation toward development moves away from the mechanistic (stimulus-organism-response) model that was predominant in behavioral psychology in the 1970's. Maslow emphasizes a more positive and humanistic approach to development that presents each person with the opportunity to develop into his or her own potential, whatever that might be.

Maslow's Hierarchy of Needs is by definition a linear model (the hierarchy is usually represented within a triangle or pyramid with Self-Actualization at its apex, but is shown here in horizontal format to allow for comparison to other stage models). It assumes that "lower" level, basic needs such as food and water are antecedent to successively higher level needs, culminating in the need to satisfy one's "highest" potential. Clearly, each successive stage is dependent on the fulfillment of the previous stage before the next stage becomes active. By comparison to the earlier models put forward by Erikson, Piaget, and Kohlberg, Maslow's model expands the more foundational, 'lower' stages and compresses the 'higher' stages. Self-Actualization comes only at the ultimate stage of development.[25]

---

24 McClelland and others developed an assessment for these needs called the Thematic Apperception Test (TAT), a projective test that presents participants with ambiguous images, and tell stories about them. The TAT methodology has been highly influential in the subsequent development of assessment instruments like many of those described below.

25 Abraham H. Maslow, *Motivation and Personality,* 2d ed., (New York: Harper and Row, 1970), 3.

Physiological	Safety	Love/Belonging	Esteem	Self-Actualization
Food, water, sleep, shelter, sex	*Physical safety, security, routine, freedom from threat*	*Love, affection, family, group membership, and acceptance*	*Achievement, recognition, status, competence*	*Creating one's highest potential, innovation, high level of awareness*

Fig. 4 — Maslow's Hierarchy of Needs

Within the needs hierarchy, Maslow identifies two different types of motivations, Deficiency and Being, which lead individuals to act to fulfill needs. Deficiency needs are motivating to the individual when he or she feels the anxiety or tension created by the need, and acts to reduce these feelings. When Deficiency needs are met or satisfied, they lose their motivational power. Being needs are always motivational by virtue of the reward the individual feels or receives as a result of action taken to meet these needs. Being needs are considered of a higher order than Deficiency needs. The goals of Being needs may never be completely fulfilled. The ultimate Being need articulated in Maslow's model is for each person to become "self-actualized"—aware of and actively pursuing the development of one's highest, and most creative potential. The satisfaction of the higher level, Being needs is not just a "nice to have" condition, but is essential for any person to live a healthy, well developed and balanced life.

Maslow's model has become highly popular and widely known. It has helped raise awareness that needs—we would equally say "values"—are motivational, and stimulate development. Maslow's hierarchy has also been very influential in codifying the idea that development is both linear and hierarchal, proceeding from 'lower' to 'higher.' This has helped foster the assumption that we must naturally seek higher levels of development and satisfaction as values progress from Deficiency to Being levels in Maslow's hierarchy.

Milton Rokeach

Milton Rokeach's concepts of Instrumental and Terminal values follow from and refine the long-standing idea that 'ends' differ from 'means.' Rokeach listed 18 values in each of the two categories, and created a survey to measure an individual's value priorities by rank order. The advantage to values theory is that it strongly suggests an individual's disposition to behavior can be observed to correspond to his or her value priorities.

While the set of 18 values in each of Rokeach's categories span most of the stages identified by authors previously discussed, Rokeach did not use a stage model. While demonstrating the importance of internal and external factors including situational influences in an individual's values rankings, Rokeach's categories pose a problem with regard to theories that place values within specific developmental or ethical stages, usually understood as hierarchal. Stage theories require that lower stage values be antecedent to and support higher stage values. Without this structure, previous developmental schemes are at a loss to explain how individuals develop. Rokeach's Terminal values, which refer to "end states of existence," and his Instrumental values, which are "values of conduct," are independent of each other.

Below are the Rokeach Terminal and Instrumental values, which form the basis for the Rokeach Value Survey.[26]

Terminal Values	Instrumental Values
A Comfortable Life	Ambitious
An Exciting Life	Broadminded
A Sense of Accomplishment	Capable
A Word of Peace	Cheerful
A World of Beauty	Clean
Equality	Courageous
Family Security	Forgiving
Freedom	Helpful
Happiness	Honest
Inner Harmony	Imaginative
Mature Love	Independent
National Security	Intellectual
Pleasure	Loving
Salvation	Logical
Self-Respect	Obedient
Social Recognition	Polite
True Friendship	Responsible
Wisdom	Self-Controlled

Fig. 5 — Rokeach's Terminal and Instrumental Values

26 Milton Rokeach, *Understanding Human Values,* (New York: The Free Press. 1973), 197.

James Fowler

Drawing from Piaget and Kohlberg, James Fowler articulates a model that identifies the development of religious faith. As in previous stage models, it is assumed that the achievement of each stage of development depends on successful attainment to the previous stages. Fowler's stages are the extension of Kohlberg's Moral Development stages, which are in turn an extension of Piaget's stages of cognitive development. However, Fowler's model expands the dynamics of development in terms of the challenges each stage of development presents to a person. Fowler also expands on the dynamics of movement from one stage to the next. For example, the movement from the values of conventional conformity characteristic of Stage 3 into the "Individuative-Reflective" values of Stage 4 is driven by an individual's growing need to take personal responsibility for his or her own actions and development. This shift tends also to be accompanied by a period of angst and struggle as previously held values are superseded and new values are tested in behavior. Individuals who have developed spiritually into the highest stages (5 and 6) operate at a greater attitudinal and behavioral distance from the earlier, conventional stages, and may even appear inscrutable or indeed threatening to people still holding perspectives supported by earlier stages.[27]

Stage 1	Stage 2	Stage 3	Stage 4	Stage 5	Stage 6
Intuitive-Projective	Mythic-Literal	Synthetic-Conventional	Individuative-Reflective	Conjunctive	Universalizing
3-7 yrs.	6-12 yrs.	12-Early Adult	Early Adult	Adult	Adult

Fig. 6 — Fowler's Stages of Faith Development

Fowler's application of stage development theory to stages of faith development, and the sometimes challenging dynamics of shift from lower to higher stages are themes that are enlarged in the work of Brian Hall and Benjamin Tonna.

Brian Hall and Benjamin Tonna

The Hall-Tonna eight-stage model and survey, called Values Technology, comprehensively synthesizes and significantly expands upon previous stage theory models. Brian Hall and Benjamin Tonna posit

27 James Fowler, *Stages of Faith*, (San Francisco: Harper and Row, 1971), 200.

125 human values, and Hall constructs a multilayered system describing the functional dynamics of values in both individual and institutional development. Hall draws heavily on several of the authors mentioned above in his book, *Values Shift*, which depends on and synthesizes their contributions to developmental theory.[28]

Hall groups the eight stages into four phases that are similar to Kohlberg's social/cognitive phases (Pre-Conventional, Conventional and Post-Conventional), each representing what Hall terms a "worldview." The four phases correspond to the External-Internal Locus of Control theory developed throughout the 1960s and 1970s.[29] Phases One and Two are characterized by the establishment of security, social membership, looking to designated authority for direction, management and achievement. Phases Three and Four are characterized by strong priorities of personal motivation, independent decision making, risk taking, interdependence and eventually stewardship at a global level.

Hall's Phase I "Surviving" worldview comprises the foundational Stages 1 and 2, which contain the values oriented toward Safety and Security respectively. The Phase II "Belonging" worldview spans Stages 3 and 4, which contain the values oriented toward Family and Institution. The Phase III "Self-Initiating" worldview comprises Stages 5 and 6, which include the values oriented toward discovering personal Vocation and creating New Order. Finally, Phase IV represents the "Interdependent" worldview of stages 7 and 8, containing the Wisdom and Global Order values.[30]

Hall and Tonna's 125 human values are unevenly distributed among the eight stages, and are most heavily concentrated toward the mid stages 4 and 5. In each stage, Hall and Tonna incorporate a variation of Rokeach's Terminal and Instrumental categories of values, renamed "Goals" and "Means." Additionally, the values in these eight stages are grouped into four other categories: Instrumental, Interpersonal, Imaginal, and Systems.[31] Development along the continuum occurs through seven cycles that overlap and connect each stage to the next. The following table is adapted from *Values Shift* and shows the basic structure of stages and developmental cycles, but we have omitted the specific values assigned to each stage.[32]

---

28 Brian P. Hall, *Values Shift*, (Rockport, MA: Twin Lights Publishers, Inc., 1995) 100.
29 Julian B. Rotter, "Generalized Expectancies for Internal Versus External Control of Reinforcement," *Psychological Monographs: General and Applied 80, no.1 (1966)* 1-28.
30 Hall, 281.
31 Ibid., 100.
32 Adapted from Hall, 160, 281.

SURVIVING		BELONGING		SELF-INITIATING		INTERDEPENDENT	
STAGE 1 *Safety*	STAGE 2 *Security*	STAGE 3 *Family*	STAGE 4 *Institution*	STAGE 5 *Vocation*	STAGE 6 *New Order*	STAGE 7 *Wisdom*	STAGE 8 *Global Order*

CYCLE 1 Safety/ Security	CYCLE 2 Security/ Family	CYCLE 3 Family/ Institution	CYCLE 4 Institution/ Vocation	CYCLE 5 Vocation/ New Order	CYCLE 6 New Order/ Wisdom	CYCLE 7 Wisdom/ Global Order
ALIEN MYSTERY *feeling vulnerable*	PROTECTED *feeling safe, belonging*	CIVIL ORDER *working to achieve success*	RELATIONAL *awareness of self and others*	CREATIVE PROJECT *individual creation*	COOPERATIVE VENTURE *collaborative creation*	GLOBAL *co-creation and caring for the world*
STYLE OF LEADER Authoritarian	Paternalistic	Manager	Facilitator	Collaborator	Servant	Visionary
COWORKER CHARACTER Oppressed	Preserver	Loyal Subordinate	Impersonal & Searching	Creative & Independent	Wise & Inter-dependent	Prophetic
ORGANIZATIONAL CHARACTER Dictatorial System	Benevolent Hierarchal System	Complex Hierarchal System	Laissez-Faire Enabling System	Collaborative System	Inter-dependent Network System	Global Convivial System

Fig 7 — Hall-Tonna Values Stages and Developmental Cycles

The work of Hall (an Anglican priest and pastoral counselor with training in psychoanalysis) and Tonna (a Catholic priest and sociologist) originates in a religious context. Like Fowler, Hall pays attention to the psychological dynamics of development from earlier to more advanced stages; indeed, the Hall-Tonna model originated in the Christian pastoral counseling background and sociological framework of the authors. Hall discusses the characteristics of the "values shift" inherent in development through successive stages, and further identifies the special implications of development from one Phase/Worldview to the next. Of particular interest is the shift from Phase II to Phase III, where the individual experiences a transformation from using an external locus of control as a guide to an internal locus of control, which can be accompanied by a sense of internal anxiety.

Hall has applied his version of the developmental model to organizations as well as individuals. The table above shows how his model, showing cycles of development from one stage to the next, is applied to leadership styles, co-worker character, and organizational character.[33]

It is clearly Hall's assumption that the cycles and stages of the continuum indicate increasing degrees of higher consciousness, (left to right across the table). In addition, the descriptions of the various styles

33 Adapted from Hall, 160.

also show similar assumptions regarding increasing degrees of emotional, intellectual, relational, and moral development. These determinations are based on the assessment of one's values as a majority fall into a particular cycle or stage, i.e., the person's stage 'focus.' Importantly, this assumed linear development is combined with the tacit evaluation that operating further and further to the right is better. For example, the better leader one is, the better co-worker one is, or the better group or organization one belongs to or is examining. The final assumption Hall makes in his work is regarding the link between values and behavior, which has been discussed since the time of the Greeks. But Hall goes further in that he also assumes that holding values that are described within a given stage or cycle also predicts competence in behaviors associated with selected values.

Although Hall's and Tonna's work is not as widely known as that of the other authors mentioned above, it stands as an important milestone in the development and use of values theory. A variant on the Hall-Tonna model and measure has been developed by Paul Chippendale, who has also demonstrated correlations between individuals' Hall-Tonna stage focus and their psychological preferences as measured by the Myers-Briggs Type Indicator.[34]

Robert Freed Bales

The work of Robert Freed Bales originally focused on understanding individual behaviors in groups. The instrument he developed is referred to by its acronym SYMLOG, which stands for "**SY**stem for the **M**ultiple **L**evel **O**bservation of **G**roups."[35] SYMLOG is not a values assessment per se, but it is included here because it is values based, and clearly links values to behavior. Further, it is a multiple rater assessment, of an entire group, and as such expands the self-assessment survey approach, which is the primary method used by all previous authors. It is a survey based on the behavioral observations of others using 26 items that assess key factors found in group behavior. The results of the survey are plotted on a "three dimensional" graph called a "Field Diagram," which is developed for each individual in a group, and in the aggregate of group members, for the group itself. The dimensions, or continua, are: Positive-Negative, Up-Down, and Forward-Backward. The observations of behavior are coded

34 Clare Colins and Paul Chippendale, *New Wisdom II: Values Based Development* (Brisbane, Australia: Acorn Publications, 1995), 19-38.

35 Robert Freed Bales and Stephen P. Cohen, *Symlog, A System for the Multiple Level Observation of Groups* (New York: Free Press, 1979), 9.

in terms of these three dimensions. It is a complex process, but one that yields rich comparisons of the different perceptual fields of each person in a group. For our purposes, it is useful to note that the dimensions that frame the three dimensional field are all evaluative, with regard to assumptions about effective behavior in groups. The items themselves also have a basis in values, for example, #12, "analytical, task oriented, problem solving," # 18 "looks up to others, appreciative, trustful," and #20 "obedient, works submissively."[36] Many of the descriptions of the 26 survey items are in fact short operational definitions of values, and are similar to values found in Maslow, Rokeach, and Hall-Tonna.

Group members rate others in the group, and their respective perceptions are tabulated and plotted against norms that are considered effective or counter-productive in terms of group behavior and leadership. This measurement in and of itself is important because many authors assume that positive or effective skills follow behavior, while SYMLOG shows that one may hold values and behave in ways that are counter-productive to leadership and group effectiveness, and are rejected by the group.

Unfortunately, the items themselves also contain elements of effective or non-effective group behavior, where in the examples above both "obedience" and "trust" are connected with submissiveness. Bales does not provide formal definitions for the values he uses except in regard to what is perceived to be normative data regarding group effectiveness.

SYMLOG is notable because it is one of the few surveys that include a measure of the perception of others' behavior. This work has extensive research supporting it, so it is also useful because it immediately supports the connection between values and behavior.

Spiral Dynamics

The work of Don Beck and Chris Cowan, based on the earlier work of psychologist Clare W. Graves, is known as Spiral Dynamics. The Spiral Dynamics model is represented as a spiral with color-identified rather than sequentially-numbered stages called ^{v}MEMEs, where the superscripted v stands for values. The ^{v}MEMEs are the basic structural elements in the model, analogous to genes in DNA, but which represent eight different worldviews, and are "a core intelligence that forms systems and directs human behavior," as well as being a framework for thinking and decision making, and a structure for interpreting life conditions.[37] These form basic,

36 Bales and Cohen, 21.

37 Don Edward Beck and Christopher C. Cowan, *Spiral Dynamics: Mastering Values,*

organizing structures that describe behavioral motivations at each cycle of development, each leading into the next in a cyclical manner, not unlike the developmental mechanism described by Piaget. The ᵛMEMEs themselves closely parallel Fowler and Hall-Tonna in their descriptions and function.

Although the form of the model attempts to avoid the rigidity of previous models, the overall antecedent/subsequent nature of development as described by the classic stage model is retained. Spiral Dynamics does not deal with individual values at the same level of specificity as other models, but instead explores the implications of the different ᵛMEMEs with regard to the life conditions described by each and the characteristic means of coping with these conditions.

BEIGE SurvivalSense	PURPLE KinSpirts	RED PowerGods	BLUE TruthForce	ORANGE StriveDrive	GREEN HumanBond	YELLOW FlexFlow	TURQUOISE GlobalView
Instinctive	*Animistic*	*Egocentric*	*Absolutistic*	*Multiplistic*	*Relativistic*	*Systemic*	*Holistic*

Fig. 8 — Beck and Cowan's Eight "Landmark" ᵛMemes

Beck and Cowan, more than previous authors and their respective models, generalize from the individual to the organization, to a society, and then to the development of humans as a species. Not that other authors do not use their models broadly, but Spiral Dynamics is more explicit about its general application than most, and this is an important contribution to values theory that has attracted serious adherents and its development is ongoing. A Coral ᵛMEME has been hypothesized that posits a stage beyond Turquoise, representing the yet-to-be described next emergent level of conscious attainment that is possible for the human species.

In spite of a large degree of specialized and evolving terminology which is used to describe stages and their inter-relationships and the mechanisms by which development occurs as well as describing how one becomes a change agent, or "spiral wizard," Spiral Dynamics remains true to the form and issues postulated by Erickson, Piaget, and Kohlberg in regard to the description of development, the process of development from one stage to another, and the nature of the objective of that development. However after Kohlberg, the assumption that values selection can be used to assess development has been largely unchallenged. Chris Cowan has commented on the cognitive and cultural difficulties inherent in the stage

---

Leadership, and Change, (Malden, MA: Blackwell Publishing, 1996), 40.

model, firmly stating that any assumption that "greatness" occurs only at the top of the spiral model is a misconception.[38]

Richard Barrett

Richard Barrett's values model describes seven stages or "levels of consciousness" applicable to both individual and groups, although the individual perspective is meant to be compared to the perspective of a group, team, or organization of which the individual is a member (Barrett specifically refers to Spiral Dynamics as an influence on this model). Barrett's levels operate hierarchically, and "evolutionarily," as do most models since Maslow's Hierarchy of Needs. Barrett's "Levels of Consciousness" are presented vertically—Level 1 is at the bottom of the Levels and Level 7 is at the top—but the similarity of his levels with most other authors reviewed before is clear. The names of the seven levels are also descriptions of the major motivator for that particular level. Barrett, like Hall, identifies three clusters of levels in the CTS model where C= Common Good, T= Transformation, and S= Self Interest.[39] The levels and their cluster designations are shown below:

Self Interest			Transformation	Common Good		
Level 1 ***Survival***	**Level 2** ***Relationship***	**Level 3** ***Self Esteem***	**Level 4** ***Transformation***	**Level 5** ***Internal Cohesion***	**Level 6** ***Making a Difference***	**Level 7** ***Service***
Physical needs	*Feeling safe, respected, loved*	*Personal self-worth*	*Freedom through releasing fears for survival, feeling loved, being respected*	*Personal meaning in existence*	*Making a positive difference in the world*	*A life of selfless service*

Fig. 9 — Summary of Barrett's Seven Levels and CTS Clusters

Barrett states that "the first three levels in the development of group consciousness represent stages in the emergence and development of the group ego (the decision making authority or leadership elite), and the last three levels represent stages in the emergence and unfolding of the group soul (the collective interest of all group members)." The level in between, Level 4, is defined as the level of "Transformation" (similar to Hall's

38 NVC Consulting, "Spiral Dynamics FAQ Caveats and Concerns," accessed January 20, 2014, http://spiraldynamics.org/faq-caveats-and-concerns/.

39 Richard Barrett, *Building a Values-Driven Organization*, (Burlingame, MA: Butterworth-Heinemann, 2006), 11-16, 38.

notion of the often psychologically and behaviorally challenging shift between his Phase II and III). This level is seen as pivotal in development, and describes a significant shift from self-interest to alignment with "the interests of all group members."[40] Significantly, Barrett also posits the existence of negative values, values that are "potentially limiting." These limiting values are based in fears that are related to the "lower levels of consciousness" of the Self Interest cluster that is, Levels 1, 2 and 3, and may lead to actions directed away from the common good. These fears are surpassed in the transformational experience of Level 4. No limiting values are found at the "upper levels of consciousness," Levels 5, 6 and 7, which by definition are directed toward the common good.[41]

Cultural Orientations: Differences and Similarities in Values

Most of the previous works reviewed so far have a distinctly psychological, and therefore basically individualistic approach that by extension may describe groups (the work of Bales being an exception, focused on group behavior first and individual secondarily). While stage models for the most part originate in successive refinements of psychological observations originally linked to phases of physical maturation beginning at infancy, cultural value models originate in observation and measurement of what exists in terms of behavior within and across groups. The aims of the two approaches are different. While stage-based models have evolved in predictive power, cultural models have evolved in descriptive power.

Shalom Schwartz

Shalom Schwartz has developed a survey that takes a primarily cultural orientation toward values. The survey called the Schwartz Value Inventory (SVI) assesses values on both an individual and cultural level of observation.[42] He uses many of the foundational theorists that the GLOBE

40 Ibid., 17.

41 Ibid., 21-22.

42 Shalom H. Schwartz, "A Theory of Cultural Values and Some Implications for Work," *Applied Psychology: An International Review* 48, no. 1, (1999), 23-47. Also, Peter B. Smith and Shalom H. Schwartz, "Values," John W. Berry, Marshall H. Segall and Cigdem Kagitçibasi (eds.), *Handbook of Cross-Cultural Psychology*, Vol.3, 2d. ed. (Boston: Allyn & Bacon, 1997) 77-118. See also: "Schwartz Value Survey" at http://

study (discussed below) depends upon, hence you will see some similarity in the general concepts, as the work of the social psychologist Geert Hofstede in particular enjoys a strong influence in intercultural studies.[43] Additionally, and importantly, Hofstede used the Rokeach survey to help validate his cultural constructs, which then set the stage for further work in regard to exploring values and culture.[44]

Schwartz identifies three basic human needs: biological needs, social interaction needs, and group survival and welfare. Based on these needs, Schwartz identifies ten "goals" comprising clusters of individual values that respond to one, two, or three of these basic human needs. The ten Motivational Goals are:

- Power
- Achievement
- Hedonism
- Stimulation
- Self-Direction
- Universalism
- Benevolence
- Tradition
- Conformity
- Security

Each Motivational Goal represents a cluster of values that are aspects of the larger Goal. For example, Equality is an expression of Universalism, and Pleasure of Hedonism.

Importantly, Schwartz observes that pursuing certain of the basic goal values requires that other basic goal values become less important, either situationally, in which case values are reprioritized at will, or attitudinally, which will predict internal (or indeed external) conflict. Schwartz describes this potential for dissonance in the relationship of seven Cultural Orientations that can be identified across cultures worldwide: Conservatism, Intellectual Autonomy, Affective Autonomy, Hierarchy, Egalitarianism, Mastery and Harmony. Schwartz observes

---

www.imo-international.de/index_englisch.htm?/englisch/html/svs_info_en.htm.

43 See Geert Hofstede, *Cultures Consequences* (Beverly Hills, Sage, 1980/2001); See also Harry C. Triandis, *Individualism & Collectivism* (Boulder, CO: Westview, 1995).

44 Geert Hofstede and Michael H. Bond, "Hofstede's Culture Dimensions: An Independent Validation Using Rokeach's Value Survey," *Journal of Cross-Cultural-Psychology* 15 (December, 1988), 417-433.

that these orientations are generally found to be in opposition to each other: Conservatism is generally seen to be in opposition to Intellectual and Affective Autonomy, Hierarchy tends to be seen in opposition to Egalitarianism, and Mastery (characterized by ambition) tends to appear in opposition to Harmony (peacefulness, unity). Nevertheless, Schwartz stresses that these orientations represent a motivational continuum best conceptualized as a circular model, such that orientations neighboring each other on the circular continuum are more similar in motivation whereas those at opposite poles of the circle are more opposed with regard to motivation. Schwartz uses this Cultural Orientations model to situate individual values choices within a universal cultural framework. This circular or "pie chart" formulation avoids the left-to-right implication of developmental hierarchy in the orientations. This is useful for a cultural approach, as the overarching goal for cultural descriptions is first an understanding of "what is." Indeed, what to do next is often a problem because approaching values from a "macro" orientation presents a challenge as to what to do with data that describes something as large and amorphous as a culture.

The Schwartz values model does supply some supporting structural conclusions, by grouping the ten Motivational Goals into four cells; Self-Enhancement, Conservation, Openness to Change, and Self-Transcendence. Here, Schwartz's model suggests some of the difficulties encountered with the use of a developmental continuum. The goals of Achievement and Power are grouped as Self-Enhancement values, Security, Conformity and Tradition are labeled Conservation values. Both of these groups are characterized as anxiety-based, concerned with protection against loss and threat. The goals of Hedonism, Stimulation and Self-Direction are labeled as Openness to Change, and the goals of Universalism and Benevolence are grouped as Self-Transcendence values. These two groups are characterized as free from anxiety, promoting gain, self-expression and growth. The emotional, and judgmental, distinction seems clear, particularly with regard to attributing the experience of anxiety or freedom from it to two clusters of values over two opposed clusters.[45]

The GLOBE Study

The result of wide reaching research regarding cultural values and leadership was completed by an international team, headed by Robert J.

45 Shalom H. Schwartz, "An Overview of the Schwartz Theory of Basic Values." Online Readings in Psychology and Culture, 2(1), December 1, 2012, accessed July 10, 2013, http://scholarworks.gvsu.edu/cgi/viewcontent.cgi?article=1116&context=orpc.

House. The study, called *The GLOBE Study Of 62 Societies*, surveyed over 17,000 middle managers from 951 organizations. The GLOBE (Global Leadership and Organizational Behavior Effectiveness) study is truly massive and primarily addresses leadership characteristics, among which are terms found in many values assessment surveys. The links between leadership and values is a fundamental aspect of the study. Indeed, the first proposition of the integrated theory on which the study is founded states, "Societal norms of shared values and practices affect leaders' behavior."[46] The GLOBE research compares assessments of what people say is actually happening in each of the countries surveyed with what people would ideally prefer.

Nine constructs are used to organize responses by country. Unlike stage theories, these constructs are validated independent factors that were built on the work of Hofstede, Schwartz, Smith, Inglehart, and others.[47] The constructs are not sequentially or hierarchically arranged and do not comprise any sort of continuum. In the course of the research, values were identified that were found to correlate with each construct. The constructs are as follows:

- Power Distance—Cultural values include: Position important, Obeying others, Deferring to elders, Inequality okay.
- Uncertainty Avoidance—Cultural values include: Orderliness and consistency, Highly structured, Detailed instructions.
- Humane Orientation—Cultural values include: Concerned about others, Sensitive toward others, Being friendly, Tolerating mistakes.
- Collective I (Institutional Collectivism)—Cultural values include: Group loyalty, Maximizing collective interests, Team sports, Team projects.
- Collective II (In-Group Collectivism)—Cultural values include: Organizational loyalty, Pride in In-Group members' accomplishments, Proud of society being positively viewed by others.

---

46 *Culture, Leadership, and Organizations: The GLOBE Study of 62 Societies*. Robert J. House et al, eds. (Thousand Oaks, CA: Sage Publications. 2004) 17.

47 A summary of the Globe study by Michael H. Hoppe, who was part of the research team, can be found at http://www.inspireimagineinnovate.com/PDF/GLOBEsummary-by-Michael-H-Hoppe.pdf.

- Assertiveness—Cultural values include: Aggressive, Dominant, Tough.
- Gender Egalitarianism—Cultural values include: Both men and women managers, Girls and boys play sports, Failure has equal consequences for men and women, Professional development equal.
- Future Orientation—Cultural values include: Planning ahead, Planning for future, Living in future, Planning meetings.
- Performance Orientation—Cultural values include: Improving performance, Rewarding performance, Being innovative, Challenging goals.

The cultural "value" definitions that support the concepts being measured are a combination of traits, behaviors and what we would call values. For example, the concept of Power Distance is assessed by the item, "Followers are (should be) expected to obey their leaders without question," which we identify as the value Obedience. Uncertainty Avoidance is assessed by the item, "Most people lead (should lead) highly structured lives with few unexpected events," which refers to several values, including Stability, Order, and Rule of Law, and would be negatively correlated with Flexibility. The concept of Assertiveness is notable because it is assessed with the item, "People are (should be) generally dominant in their relationships with each other."[48] This item and the associated definition includes the concepts of dominance and aggression within the concept of Assertiveness, which is a common use of the term, but runs counter to the literature that deals with assertiveness as being neither specifically passive nor aggressive in its concept or in its associated behaviors.

The study found that six global leadership styles could be identified as common to all country respondent groups. These styles are "referred to as culturally endorsed, implicit theories of leadership (CLT). That is, members of the cultures share common observations and values concerning what constitutes effective and ineffective leadership." The six global styles are:

- Charismatic/Value Based leadership
- Team Oriented leadership
- Participative leadership

---

48 House, et al. 30.

- Autonomous leadership
- Humane-Oriented leadership
- Self-Protective leadership.[49]

The GLOBE study is rich in findings, but it must be remembered that extending group (cultural) findings to specific individuals is never supported without the individual going through some sort of self-assessment process, and then a self-validation process that allows comparison between the social level and the individual level of observation. The immediate utility of the GLOBE study in regard to this book is a confirmation that indeed, values can be identified and assessed in terms of behavior, which in the case of the GLOBE study is leadership behavior.

World Values Survey (WVS)

This is a survey, repeated at five year intervals, which assesses values, attitudes toward particular issues, and states of being (like happiness), but it is not strictly limited to values. The results of the survey are reported by country, the scope of which has grown to include over 60 countries, and the last assessment included over 90,000 respondents. On April 1, 2014 the sixth round of data will be released, spanning a 30 year time period, which provides a remarkable amount of data regarding the overall values and the trends in the respective countries and their various groupings.[50] The reported data is, like the GLOBE study, a report of "what is," which leaves the issue of development a challenge to be answered by each person, manager, or policy maker. In addition to answering survey questions, each respondent must provide information giving context (cultural, situational, and individual) as well as provide his or her behavioral applications for a given value.

Perhaps one of the most interesting and, for our purposes, most useful results of the WVS is the Inglehart-Welzel Cultural Map. This is a graphic representation of countries as they cluster on two dimensions. The vertical dimension identifies a Traditional/Secular-Rational values continuum, and the horizontal dimension identifies a Survival/Self Expression values continuum. This map and its various dimensions in regard to trends in democratization are fully described by Ronald Inglehart and Christian

---

49 Ibid., 496.

50 World Values Survey, accessed January 14, 2014, http://www.worldvaluessurvey.org/.

Welzel in a paper available on the WVS website.[51] A great deal of additional research and support information is freely available at the site.

For our uses, this map provides partial face validity for the values continuum identified by many authors, along the Survival/ Self Expression dimension. This map is potentially useful in both individual and organizational development situations (especially in multi-national organizations or those organizations that operate in a multicultural environment) as a point of comparison for similarities and specific, situational differences, because it provides an empirically grounded perspective.

Finally, the Ingelhart and Welzel paper identifies and discusses the predictive ability of group values in regard to democratization, which helps to clarify how values, at the group level only, can predict behavior. However, we must also recognize that the massive numbers of subjects well qualifies the statistical requirements for sufficiency, and that since values are so extremely ambiguous, it is not possible to extrapolate from group values data to a single or even a small group of individuals.

As was mentioned above, The World Values Survey addresses more than values identification and assessment, so it is not surprising that it also uses a variety of items structured in different ways to assess the values of an individual as he or she represents a given culture. We include it here because it offers an excellent example of current values research which, while different in its fundamental nature from the individual stage models reviewed above, is comparable to the GLOBE study, focusing at the level of culture rather than individual.

Conclusion

Our intent in this review is to show from where values theory has originated, as well as give you a general idea of how it has grown and been extended. We have briefly noted some of the major and minor authors that have dealt with values and their explanation, or theory. There are several important points we need to mention that run throughout these authors' writings. The first is that values theory has become more robust,

51 Ronald Inglehart and Christian Welzel, "Changing Mass Priorities: The Link between Modernization and Democracy," *Perspectives on Politics*, 121 no. 2 (June 2010), 551-567, accessed January 15, 2014, http://www.worldvaluessurvey.org/wvs/articles/folder_published/publication_587/files/ChangingMassPriorities.pdf.

more technical, and more complicated, particularly in the past 25 years. The second is to show that values can be arranged stage-wise, along continua generally ranging from more basic and survival-focused to more expansive and globally focused.

There are various ways in which values might be arranged along a continuum, and various reasons for doing so. In regard to values at the level of individual experience, there exists a near consensus among writers regarding the continuum-array of values, and the terms used to describe it. The major stages that mark different orientations, levels of development or worldview are not exactly the same for every author, but there is a great deal of parallel thinking in regard to what constitutes these stages. We have shown that most authors have assumed that these stages coincide with human developmental stages (i.e., birth to fully-attained adult awareness), and that this view is widely accepted and used.

Our own experience has shown us that, values indeed tend to cluster and link together, as we will discuss in Part III, and that clustering can occur for a variety of reasons. One of the ways in which values can be seen to cluster is with regard to stage characteristics, of the kinds we have seen proposed by the authors examined above. Problematically, however, there is little empirical evidence that supports exactly how a stage should be defined, and what values might be associated with it. The consensus around this gives researchers a good place to start, but work needs to be done.

Finally, there are culturally oriented approaches that consider values from a group or societal perspective, and which provide a contrasting perspective to the individualistic or psychologically oriented theory that represents the majority of work done. However, there are valuable insights that these studies and authors provide, and perhaps most importantly for our use, there are genuine points of comparison and even overlap between the two approaches.

So far, so good. Now we get to more difficult points. For the most part, the developmental continuum we see in the work of authors theorizing about individuals' values describes moral development. Although the overt reference to morality has been dropped by many authors, is still tacitly operational. Here are the problems that we see with this approach to values:

The Conflation of Concepts

As indicated above, the majority, if not all, values models and assessments that are based on a general stage model fail to differentiate between morality, emotion, intellect, rationality, personality type or preference, and cognitive style. We argue that the lack of clarity in differentiating between the assessment of values and some sort of human development is the major problem. While there may be valid correlations between values selections and some of the concepts discussed above, their assessment must be separate from that of values assessment. As mentioned above, some research exists to show correlations between, for example, personality preference and values stages, but much more needs to be done. Without clear separation, when an assessment is done, the results are, at best, confused, and are potentially misleading.

The above models also conflate age development with moral development and imply emotional development at the same time; and in the case of Kohlberg—the influence of whose work cannot be overestimated—rational development. While it seems convenient to assume these developmental concepts track with each other, we have seen in our own practice, in the work of Howard Gardner with his Multiple Intelligence theory, and Daniel Goleman's work with Emotional Intelligence, that humans often develop at different rates relative to age, emotional awareness, moral confirmation, and other factors. We have seen more than a few senior level leaders, with many years of experience and possessing high levels of rational, intellectual, and technical competence, behave with the moral and emotional maturity of a poorly developed child. It is quite possible to develop along one or two of the above dimensions, and not along others.

A sub-point to this observation is that values may be related to behavior, but not in such a causal way as to indicate either what behavior will be shown, nor the skill or competence with which the behavior will be executed. In short, one may select "high level" values because of a variety of reasons, and not be able to actually behave according to those values at all. Indeed, this is generally the case with those values that we may identify as aspirational, which are, simply put, the values we would like to be able to exercise in the best of all possible worlds we may imagine. That these values tend to remain visionary rather than actualized is not a bad thing in and of itself. Rather, it is one of the mechanisms that accomplish growth and development.

Our point is that one's selection of values does not necessarily signify behavior. It might, or it might not. We strongly suggest that the conscious expression or selection of values is not the appropriate means to measure development. However, and this begs a question of supporting research which to our knowledge has not been done, we do hypothesize that operational values would correlate with developmental stages, if an appropriate means of measuring development were identified and carefully used.

Judgment

Whether implied or explicit, stage models and instruments comprise a judgment with regard to the attainment to each successive stage. "Higher" (or typically, farther to the right on the continuum, showing a left-right language/reading bias) is clearly considered as being more well developed, implying greater awareness, and perhaps even carries, as in Fowler, and Hall-Tonna, a conclusion of somehow more advanced spiritual development.

The assessment of moral development is a difficult thing to do. The presumption is that the observer, or the survey, can stand in a position of judgment without recognizing the moral bias of the assessment that is operating in an a priori manner. Morality can only be held by a social group. Its origin is not an individual, creative product. While the establishment of this sort of judgmental position may not be what various authors intend with their individual contributions, it nevertheless is where this general stage-developmental model leads.

But, that is not actually the most important part of this issue. The important part is safety. The key to all successful developmental facilitation, a principle that is commonly voiced as the single most important issue, is, "Create a safe place, then get out of the way." Physical, psychological (which includes emotional and intellectual), and social safety are the absolute requirements for people to actually begin the process of self-reflection and consider the possibility of allowing for change. And there is nothing more anxiety-inducing than the possibility of being judged. Because everyone knows, we will always be found wanting when that judgment is finished.

We have brought this point up, in regard to the use of values instruments that imply or state judgments, to consultants who use them, and each time, every time, we have received the same answer. "But that is not the way I use it." To which we say, "Nonsense." People are not stupid, and in nearly any modern organization, they are trained, and are highly motivated, to achieve. Stage models hold up an end goal, a highest stage, and say in many different ways, "Go here." This is where developed, (or enlightened, mature, intelligent, spiritual, etc.) people have gone, and you are being compared to them." So people respond powerfully to the underlying promise offered by stage models. The drive toward achievement of the most-desired state is built-in to the conceptual models and assessment reports based on those models, and if put into operation with an individual or organization, speak for themselves.

Development, as we are using the term, refers to psycho-social growth which results in change that is directed toward an end state, such as maturity, wisdom, or spiritual enlightenment. So there is a question about the use of a child development model as being analogous to adult learning. We will not even attempt to summarize the differences, but simply point out that foundational values approaches like Piaget and Kohlberg are describing child development which is marked by discontinuous stages, that is, that a stage of development proceeds from an event in life such as the first step or first words. There does exist a large body of literature and supporting research that disagrees with the traditional, hierarchical, linear, discontinuous stage model. Some argue for a continuous developmental model, while others argue for an overlapping wave model where development occurs sometimes sequentially, and at other times in overlapping processes, but in the form of increasing or decreasing waves.[52]

We are not against development. However, we find the stage model with its implications to be neither useful nor acceptable vis-à-vis values. And the use of a developmental stage model raises a legitimate question regarding the ethics of assessing someone's standing in regard to a prescribed developmental location which places the observer or assessment in a place of judgment, particularly of moral judgment, of the person in question.

As with any theory or model—ours or anyone else's—we suggest caution regarding strict and literal interpretations. So, before you think we are discarding the above work, let us clearly advise not to 'throw out the baby with the bath water.' The concepts that stages represent are useful, even though the word "stage" carries connotations that lead to difficulties when using it. The idea of a category is useful in grouping values together in regard to a governing concept, which is something that can be used without judgment. We have decided to use the term "Perspective" to denote these categories, as we think it is more accurate, and does not carry the same connotation as "stage." What matters in regard to values is not the attainment of a stage of development, particularly given these stages, while useful, are little understood in practice; rather, what perspective does the individual take on what is most important to her, and how can he or she best reflect and act on values choices given her life context.

---

52 Thomas Keenan, and Subhadra Evans, *An Introduction to Child Development*, 2nd. ed. (Thousand Oaks, CA: Sage, 2009), 7.

There are many insights into the characteristics and dynamics of values that can be learned and applied. To that end we have built on these authors, and are suggesting a more careful examination of values theory. Our objective is to present a similar model, but one that is more simply, and hopefully, more carefully described given what we know after centuries of thinking on values.

Finally, the cultural orientation to values is important to recognize, but is not as useful for the more individualistic psychological approach because in the cultural approach one is, at best, comparing how he or she relates to the more general values held by a culture or society. While that sort of comparison may be interesting it will likely not result in much personal insight regarding how one might understand his or her choices and behaviors, or what options might be available if intentional changes were desired.

Part III: Describing and Organizing Values

Values and how they work have a number of characteristics. Many of these characteristics have been identified in the work of scholars and researchers (as briefly reviewed above). We rely too on our own experience working with many individuals and groups, helping them both assess and develop their values and the systems that hold those values, as well as helping them to better implement their values.

There are thousands of potential human values (this is one characteristic of values). For that reason, we will not attempt to dive into an in-depth discussion of single values and their definitions. It is much more useful to clarify concepts and characteristics that describe how values work. This, in turn, will help us suggest an organizing structure for values, and most importantly, it will lead to some interpretive guidelines for dealing with values. However, it is important to provide a succinct definition of values:

A value is a human quality, arranged or structured by relative priority, or importance, and manifested through language and behavior.

Our values are always operating in the way we view the world and the choices we make. Basically, working with values makes it possible for us to keep track of what is important to us. We use and depend on values all of the time. Since they are so much a part of life, it is likely that we have not taken the time to really look at what our values a to consider how they actually work in our lives. But, it is nece take some time to understand them if we are going to use the each of us may define a good life; or the best life we may ven life context and circumstances.

rally, values provide the means for us to select from and interpret in our environment and make choices about how to respond to e stimuli. Values provide a way to make sense of what we encounter. hey also represent the sources of energy that motivate our behaviors. So understanding how values work is not only important, it gives us tools with which to work with values more effectively.

Values are identifiable through language, and to get a careful understanding of how values work, we have to consider the very language we use. James Powell suggests that we all have two sets of language. The external set is the one we use with others and is highly influenced by our interactions in the external world. The second set is internal, the language we use within our own minds. Our internal language is still a function of our external language, particularly our primary language or mother-tongue, but our internal language provides us with a sense of autonomy from our social connections. "It is within this interior language that we are able to break away from the fixed outer language," says Powell.[53] This internal place is where we can reflect on what is important, evaluate ideas or anything else, and actually hold an internal dialogue of sorts about what is important to us. It is there that we ultimately find our own world of values. Brian Hall says that, "Values mediate a human being's inner and outer worlds, and enable us to express our inner selves outwardly in our daily activities."[54] In this way, values act as a sort of bridge from between our internal and external worlds.

It is precisely because values belong to our internal, personal language that we can get so upset when we think they are being challenged or when we think that someone is trying to impose their values on us. We consider our internal selves, which includes our internal language, as reserved, and even sacred, a sort of place where only we and selected others are allowed. One challenge with this inner world and its language is finding how to work with it in a direct and useful way. In our coaching, where we use our Values Perspective Survey, much of the initial conversation is about questions like, "You have selected (name of a value. e.g., Respect) as a high priority value for you. What does that look like in your life, at work and/or away from work?" The responses give a glimpse into the internal language of that person, and with that glimpse insights emerge into the

---

53 James N. Powell, *The Tao Of Symbols* (New York: Quill. 1982), 35.

54 Hall, 35.

light of conscious examination, allowing the individual to re-assess that value, perhaps revalidating it, re-assigning it a priority place among his values, or recognizing that a different value may now be most important.

The objective of identifying the basic characteristics of values is to help you come to a better understanding of your own values, and make better judgments and decisions about what to do to grow and develop in regard to your own values. With that in mind, there are several characteristics that operate as first principles describing both what values are and how they function that are useful for our work here.

Characteristics of Values

1. Values represent energy that moves us.
2. Values are identifiable through our language and behavior.
3. The same value can mean different things to different people.
4. The meaning of most values is social and comes from interaction with others.
5. We can choose our values.
6. There are thousands of human values; and we tend to focus on a few.
7. Values do not exist in isolation, but always link or cluster together.
8. Values operate in dynamic priority or rank order. That order can change, depending on the situation.
9. Our values tell us how we *should* behave.

These characteristics are explained as follows:

1. Values represent energy that moves us. The names of values, for example, Duty, are symbolic representations of concepts and behaviors that are important for us, whether we are consciously aware of them or not. Simply hearing the name of a value can trigger the energy associated with it and we respond in a particular way (as you without doubt did, reading the value name, Duty, above) that is both culturally influenced and deeply individual. Using language that contains value words with other people has a similar effect. What sorts of energy are we talking about? Many kinds: intellectual, physical ('gut' reaction), emotional, and/or spiritual, that motivates our choices and actions. Further, the values we hold act as a filter on our perceptions, our memories, and the way we understand. We do not operate like passive recorders of information like a camera. We select what to pay attention to and actively interpret what we perceive, and our values act as a selective mechanism in this process. They work with our senses, no matter what our physical abilities may be, to help us create an understanding of the world that makes sense to us.

We never exist without values. There is no neutral state of being without values in operation. We are all born into a world of values regardless of our individual circumstances. We all have a host of sources of values that we inherit or learn very quickly in life including those that are influenced by nationality, first language, religion, the political, social, and economic situation of our families, just to name a few. And all of these sources carry values that we often accept without question, at least when we are small. We can learn to manage our values, but we cannot ever be in a value-less state. This is simply part of being human.

We understand the world, our world, from the perspective of our values whether we are aware of it or not. Sourced by the energy they encapsulate, the values we hold most closely are at the heart of why we do what we do. Politicians and advertisers know this characteristic very well and manipulate it freely. Becoming conscious of your values allows you to take advantage of knowing about this source of energy for your own benefit.

2. Values are identifiable through our language and behavior. Because they are internal drivers, values themselves are intangibles, so the only way we can actually grasp them is through language and/or behavior. What I say and do tends to reveal to any observer over time what my highest priority values are. Structured surveys are useful in providing various ways for us to examine values and their definitions, allowing us to consciously identify those values that are most important for us. At the same time, it is important to note that having a value does not guarantee our competence with regard to the skills that are required to live that value effectively. Also, there is always a wide range of possible behaviors that can reasonably be said to exemplify a single value. Others can see what values we hold by observing our behavior. Of course, we may also hold values we are not capable of actualizing through our day-to-day behavior. Still, if others are listening, they will hear those values as well.

3. The same value can mean different things to different people. A word is ambiguous when it has multiple meanings or interpretations. All language is somewhat ambiguous in this way, given each person's unique experiences and sense-making structures. Values definitely operate in this way. A given value will be somewhat differently defined by different people, and different people will live out their values through behaviors that might not be recognizable by someone else as expressing the same value. Many of those behaviors are guided by cultural norms, and by how they combine or cluster with other values. For example, the behaviors motivated by the value of *honesty* might look one way when observed in a West African village headman, who is also brought up to value *community harmony*, than when observed, say, in a female attorney raised in the western United States, who will also have been taught from childhood to value *individualism*. (More about how values cluster below.) The same pertains to groups and organizations.

Ultimately, it is up to each person and group to refine the meaning of what a particular value means to them and what kinds of behaviors signify the fulfillment of that value in action. For each individual, how any value is defined is always likely to be just a little different from how others define it. This does not mean that the meaning of values is totally subjective, only that we change the standardized or dictionary meaning of any given value anyway, so it is our responsibility to come to our own, and with others, common, understanding of the words we use to name values.

4. The meaning of most values is social, and comes from interaction with others. While their meanings may have different shadings to each of us, nevertheless the meaning of values originates in human interaction, not simply the result of personal will, need, or desires. Beyond the most basic foundational or survival values, the ones that are closest to biological needs (think of the most foundational level of Maslow's Hierarchy of Needs), how we identify our priorities is the result of living in societies and organizations. We are not usually aware of the tacit process by which our entire society is in a continual state of negotiating the actual meanings of values. This phenomenon becomes clear, however, when a group of people get together to discuss what their common operating values might be, also known as "how we do things here." While it is difficult enough to come up with a short list, the real surprise is often when someone in the group suggests a definition for one of the agreed upon values, and somebody else says, "That's not what it means to me"—a statement that is often met with a short silence followed by the contributions of several people at the same time. When working with values in groups, members need to agree on clear definitions and representative behaviors.

5. We can choose our values. As individuals or groups, we can choose to emphasize any value we want. We can intentionally choose values we do not currently hold, and we can intentionally let other values go. It is important to recognize that this is not a simple or superficial process. It requires a great deal of attention, energy, and practice. Nevertheless, values are not absolute within us. Values are subject to both rational and emotional influences, to cognitive and psychological predispositions, and to life experiences. All of these factors combine in most people to cause them to move to different values over the course of a lifetime, whether consciously or not. By the way, philosophers and psychologists, particularly those who have utilized stage models for development, until very recently have tended to suggest that emotionally driven values choices are indicative of a 'lower' state of moral and/or cognitive development and that rational choices are always 'higher.' We and others disagree.[55] Both influences always play an active role in our values choices. However, there is obviously a stronger link between survival emotions and survival values, which implies that in times of great stress, we may quickly ignore our ability to choose values and simply prioritize our values based on emotional survival impulses.

6. There are thousands of human values and we tend to focus on a few. You may come across various lists of values that have been compiled by scholars and researchers only to find that some of your own values are not there. Do not be alarmed. There are literally thousands of possible human values. Many of the terms we use to describe values are close synonyms, and some are combinations of several more specific values. As our physical and social world changes, different values may be called for. What is important in working with values assessment and development is that a person or organization has enough values choices to work with, and that those choices represent a full range of developmental possibilities. That sort of choice usually requires an initial list that is quite long (the minimum number may be a matter of debate), but we quickly find that as individuals, we really only need to identify 6-9 values to describe most of what is important to us, while 15-20 values can provide a rather complete description.

7. Values do not exist in isolation, but always link or cluster together. People simply do not hold just one value at a time. Any given value naturally links and connects to another, or other values. They may be grouped and linked in a variety of ways, but one value will always associate with others. These linkages or groupings may be determined by

---

55 Especially those who take into account relatively recent re-evaluations of evidence of the significance of emotion in the human brain and cognition; See Antonio Damasio, *The Feeling of What Happens: Body, Emotion and the Making of Consciousness* (London: Heinemann, 1999). And Daniel Goleman, *Emotional Intelligence* (New York: Bantam Books, 1995).

themes, where one value seems to be necessarily associated with another, for example, many people associate the values of Integrity and Honesty; or by what seems a natural supportive progression where one value provides the awareness and skills needed for a subsequent value, as for example can be the case for the value of Trust which may be considered to be dependent on the value of Respect.

There are also situational influences that affect how values cluster. Values always operate in a context, comprising all the factors that operate on and around one's life situation. The general context within which each of us lives powerfully affects our mindset or worldview, and we carry multiple tacit assumptions and values that are held within the larger context around us at any given time. So, to a great degree that context affects how we define a particular value. In short, values are subject to situational influences, which do make for some difficulty in their assessment.

Nevertheless, we are not absolutely bound to particular value structures. You and I are free to link or group various values together simply because such an association makes sense, or works for us. This general characteristic allows us to create structures with which to keep track of our values to help us understand how they operate in our lives, often those structures are social, like belonging to a political or religious group, which provides reinforcement for the connections we make at an individual level.

8. Values operate in dynamic priority or rank order. That order can change, depending on the situation. The order of our values is actually a structure, and the most important value or values at the top of our own priority list tends to determine the overall nature of our behavior for as long as that value occupies that position. All other values are in effect 'colored' by our highest-priority value(s), and other values that are a little less important tend to support the top priorities. However, as the situation changes, the ranking may also change. When that happens, a different value takes the top spot and begins to be the dominant influence in behavior, at least for a while. Without understanding this, we might think people are behaving inconsistently, when they are actually just adapting to different situations.

9. Values are prescriptive. They tell us how we *should* behave. Value choices are at the heart of moral and ethical behavior. All countries have laws that prescribe how we should behave. To the degree that we identify with a culture or institution, we behave not only according to the laws, but also according to the "shoulds" of that culture. Because of this characteristic, if we know what a person's or group's values genuinely are, we can predict,—not perfectly of course— with some degree of certainty how that person or group will behave when faced with a choice between behaviors that represent their values and behaviors that do not reflect those values. Value choices also tend collectively to be reflective of one or another worldview such as those described by some of the writers mentioned above. Seen through this practical lens, values are predictive of the attitudes and behaviors that have been observed as characteristic of people who hold these worldviews.

This in no way suggests that a person is not able to exercise his or her own freedom of choice and override cultural prescriptions. We are always able to do that. However, societies tend to guard their own integrity by excluding those who consistently refuse to maintain cultural codes and norms. The latitude allowed for individual choice varies with each culture. Each culture falls somewhere along a continuum identified at one end as "Collective," where values prescriptions are relatively strict and behavioral choice is somewhat limited, to "Individualistic," where tolerance for variant interpretations of values is greater, and wider behavioral tolerance is greater as well.[56] But even in individualistic cultures (think Australia and the United States), cultural norms operate in a prescriptive way which is often tacit, subtle, and powerful.

The above set of characteristics is not intended to be complete, but does begin to inform you about values. The descriptions in the above characteristics can begin to form a set of corresponding, operating assumptions about values, and how the Values Perspective model and survey reports operate and can be interpreted.

The Values Perspective Model: An Organizing Structure

One useful way to understand values is to recognize that they never operate in isolation. That is, values tend to group or link together somehow, so presenting them within some sort of model or structure is consistent with the nature of values. Historically, organizing values into a stage continuum such as those put forward by Erikson, Maslow, Kohlberg, and Hall, has given us the advantage of being able to place human values in a developmental context of succeeding perspectives. The disadvantage,

56 The Collective–Individual continuum is one of five major dimensions identified by Geert Hofstede. The others are Power Distance, Masculinity versus Femininity, Uncertainty avoidance, Long-term versus short-term orientation, Indulgence versus Restraint. See Hofstede and Bond, 417-433.

of course, is that the stage model appears to impose a linear, 'one-way' directionality on development. The number of groups, stages, or levels assigned to the continuum seems to be somewhat arbitrary (ranging, in the models discussed above, from six to nine). The more important issue is not the number of stages there might be in a developmental continuum, but that the stage-continuum is inherently hierarchal.

In our own work, we have often encountered resistance to the suggestion that a person's values, represented along a left-to-right or lower-to-higher arrangement represents some sort of evaluation or judgment, relative to where any person's main focus may be determined to fall along that continuum. For most of the authors and models presented above, particularly the psychologically grounded models, that implied judgment is an underlying part of the model, and is experienced as such whether intended or not. Development can be effectively described with a linear model if one is describing large groups of people. But, individuals do not proceed in lockstep fashion along our or anyone else's continuum. People's growth does not proceed in an orderly and predictable fashion from lower to higher stages of development. Indeed, development includes gaps and reversals, and is influenced by rigorously researched and described factors such as cognitive and personality preferences. We have worked with many highly-functioning people whose behavior provides evidence contradicting what traditional developmental theory seems to indicate. We have seen highly intelligent people (many of them executives in large organizations) behave in emotionally immature ways. We have seen people whose usual focus is on immediate family and local social norms and obligations take actions that put the wellbeing of strangers first, sometimes to the consternation of those nearest to them, and so on. These are not isolated cases; in fact, they are fairly common. You may be thinking of a few familiar examples in your own experience as you read this.

We do find the stage models instructive and in many respects are building upon the work of previous modelers. At the same time, we contend that values development is not necessarily connected with age, although we agree that biological and age development tend to support values development. That is, early years and early stages do correspond in many ways. The major difference in how we interpret the stage continuum is that we view it in terms of the *perspective* of the individual, not in terms of the *development* of the individual. The difference is significant because when one's primary focus is seen as an orientation, as one's core and the focus from which all other values and values stages are accessible, rather than the result of some kind of developmental imperative, an individual's core perspective ceases to be subject to judgmental evaluation regarding how "highly" developed one's values might be. Otherwise, the question always seems to arise, "Am I good (i.e., highly developed) enough?" or the conclusion, "Look at how good (i.e., highly developed) I am!" Both of which immediately halt the potential for genuine development at a complete impasse. Whereas, a *perspective* orientation immediately leads to questions like, "Look what I can see from here." And of course, when other perspectives are considered, "I wonder what I am missing as seen from these other perspectives." More on perspectives later, but each has its advantages and limitations.

As we mentioned earlier, even the term "stage" carries with it a connotation of development-as-imperative: if there is a stage 1 there must be a stage 2, which implies some sort of developmental change that is necessarily hierarchical, a higher stage always being somehow better than a lower. Indeed, the practical reservations many people express with regard to the traditional stage model, center on just this point. We find the notion of developmental hierarchy to be simply inaccurate, and contend that *a different perspective does not imply a more well developed or a more moral person.* On a practical level, the determination of another person's moral, emotional, relational, or even intellectual development based on a self-assessment inventory is, in our opinion, impossible. What can be measured, in regard to a values assessment, is a record and grouping of the choices people make as they are presented with the opportunity to prioritize one value over others. The overall grouping of this selection process can be identified as a point-of-view, a perspective through which we tend to view the world, and through which we tend to make the choices that drive our actions.

The Values Perspective model does not suggest, nor does the survey assess, development. Additionally, it is not a personality test, nor a psychological test of any sort. What do the model and survey describe and assess? The answer is the Values Perspective model and survey identifies priorities and a general perspective based on conscious choices regarding the values an individual says are the most important for him or her.

We use the term "Perspective" for two reasons. First, and most importantly, it more accurately represents what the model actually represents and what the survey measures, which is one's conscious identifications of priorities, and second, it avoids the misrepresentation of the implied idea that one position or perspective along the continuum is more well developed, or "better than" a different perspective. After a person is aware of his or her priorities and perspective, then questions and conversations about development may be appropriate.

The Value Perspectives are as follows:

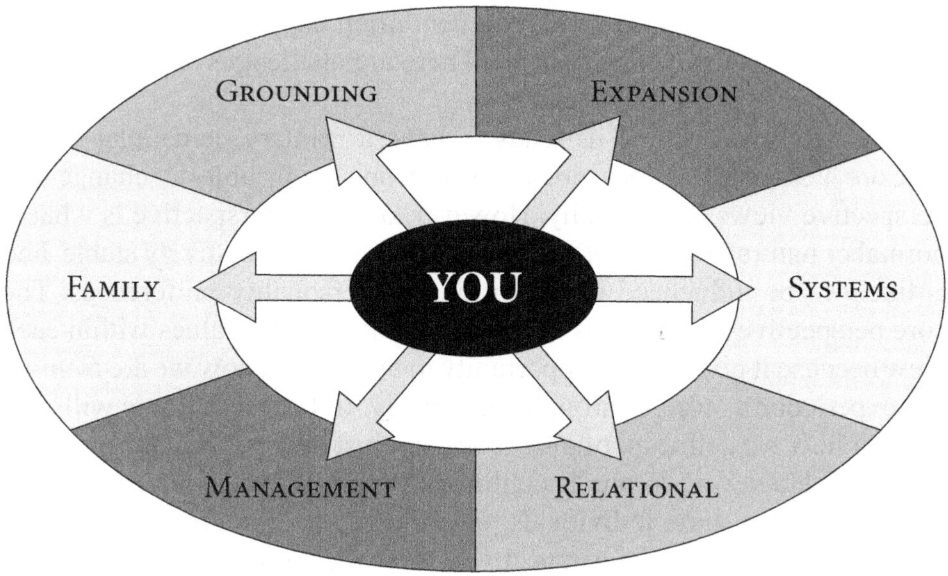

Fig. 10 - The Values Perspective Model

The above model, arranged as a circle, helps to avoid falling immediately into the inferences that plague most of the earlier models discussed above. However, the perspectives are indeed arranged along a continuum. What we have determined is that this continuum represents shifts of perspective from needing and valuing stability (i.e., Grounding) through perspectives of widening scope and increasing potential for dynamism, culminating in the dynamism and global breadth of the Expansion perspective values. The two major factors propelling shifts between perspectives are narrow scope/broad scope, and stability/dynamism. These forces are not inherently unidirectional, for example, from narrow toward broad scope. The contexts that operate in and around the lives of individuals (and in the life cycle of groups) may cause them to broaden or to narrow scope in what they value at a given time of life, likewise, to value stability over dynamism for compelling and healthy reasons. These two factors will be discussed more fully in Part IV.

Each perspective is a worldview and may act as a central focus, becoming what we refer to as the values perspective core, for any individual or group. It represents a particular outlook on the world. We do not suggest that one person's challenges are in some way greater than, or more profound, or more important than another's depending on a core perspective. That would be equivalent to saying one person's values are somehow better than another person's values, which would be absurd, but this sort of comparison and judgment often happens when people are not managing their own tendencies. There are challenges and advantages associated with every perspective.

The fact that each of us tends to have a primary perceptual frame, or Core Perspective, does not keep us from being able to change our perspective views occasionally. However, our core perspective is what is normal or natural for each of us. That core tends to be relatively stable, and is likely to be influenced by cognitive and personality preferences. The core perspective is at least as important as the specific values within each view because it gives us the opportunity to understand how we are *framing* our experience as we go through a given day. In fact, that frame will tend to color how we define all of our values, not just the ones contained within that view. However, no one is confined to a single viewpoint. It can also be the case that some individuals' or groups' attention and priorities are divided between two core perspectives. (We will discuss this situation and other issues regarding the dynamics of values in Part IV.)

We all hold and may draw on values from within any of the perspectives. Having a core perspective does not keep us from accessing any of the values that might be associated with any other perspective. A small number of highest-priority values tend to appear in a ranked order that reflects what we hold to be most important at a given time. Values tend to arrange themselves in a priority order, even though situations may require a re-ordering from time to time. The rank order is dynamic, and depends on situational needs, but the core perspective is relatively stable. It can and does change depending on both our own individual development and the general situations in which we find ourselves, but those changes usually occur more slowly than the rank ordering of specific values. For example, professionals around age 40 may have a well-established Management core perspective, which is not adequately functional to their life circumstances if they suddenly find themselves parents. Their shift to a Family core perspective may be quite dramatic with the birth of a first child. That sort of shift can be uncomfortable at times, at least until people settle into their new "home." Similarly, a young and idealistic student whose values perspective has been Expansion may need to make the effort required to shift energy toward the Management perspective in order to obtain and hold a job, perhaps long enough to solidify the influence currency that would enable a shift back toward Expansion, if the passion for it is sustained in some way. Such changes are often noticeable in the way people describe how they see the world after such a shift occurs. The shifts described above would mark a contraction in a person's scope of awareness, at least for a few years, and we suggest that shift is both appropriate and healthy.

The Core Perspective is important in another way as well. We use our core as a way to define everything else around us. We can see this best when we look at how values are expressed in our language. There are several ways in which any word can carry meaning, and values are no exception. The "denotative meaning" is usually defined as the meaning found in a dictionary. This is straightforward when the word is a noun, and refers to a physical object. But in fact, when dictionaries are compiled, the editors spend a great deal of time comparing all available dictionaries, and coming up with a sort of generic, common, or standard meaning. There is also an additional, more subjective or psychological meaning called "connotative meaning." That is the flavor or spin that you and I put on words based on our own experience and understanding of the word. Values are like this too, in that we all have our own variations on the basic definition and meaning of a value, and it is our own core perspective that forms the basis for this individual, or connotative, meaning that we use when we talk about our own values. This dynamic works the same with groups and larger organizations as well. In those cases, the connotative meaning is part of the group or organizational culture and is part of "the way we do things here." We notice it when we are new to a group or organization. After we have learned the jargon, and incorporated it, we forget our first encounter with its strangeness. When we lose our awareness of it, we have likely internalized both the organizational culture and the actual, operational values associated with it. (We recognize those actual organizational values are often different from the values that are codified by organizational leaders as those values which *should* guide employees.) A perspective worldview operates very much like that organizational culture: not only does it become familiar, but it becomes the way the world should look, at least to us.

Below are the descriptions of each perspective, including some of the specific values associated with each. Keeping in mind that there are thousands of human values, please remember that those listed below are by no means not the only possible values that can be associated with a given perspective.

Grounding Perspective

The Grounding Perspective always operates as support to the individual, group, organization, or society. It is concerned with security and safety. Many Grounding values could be labeled "species survival" values, and as such they can even be said to be to some extent genetic in origin. They are that basic. So the values of this view are extremely important, and they represent goals that require skills that by a certain point in the course of physical development are usually already being met in a regular and predictable way. This will generally be the case for a majority of people in developed countries or anywhere that basic needs can be met through securely accessible means. These values are recognizably similar to the physiological needs at the base of Maslow's needs hierarchy, and include concerns with regard to basic functioning. Many, but not all, are physically oriented. Because of this, adults often do not generally focus their conscious, daily energy in the Grounding perspective, since the values belonging to this perspective and the skills associated with them that satisfy basic life needs should already be in place. Thus, Grounding values can operate "in the background" without much attention, until some stress or crisis focuses our attention on them. However, when that occurs, it is extremely important that we do have the ability to exercise these values. Types of stress which may trigger a return to focus in the Grounding perspective include chronic illness or serious injury, abrupt change in status like job loss or the death of a close loved one, financial loss, or conscious attention to foundational issues such as addiction. But the stresses do not have to be negative. The birth of a child, for example, a wonderful event for most parents, can easily trigger the need to stress Grounding values; a job promotion may trigger similar reactions, but for still different reasons.

When we see the world from within the viewpoint of the Grounding perspective, daily challenges are often perceived to be imposed upon us, so we can feel ourselves to be in a primarily reactive mode. It is unlikely that we are able to assume (or to believe we can assume) much responsibility for our actions and may find ourselves in a position of having very limited control of our situation. It may seem to us that life is determined by fate or destiny, and can often be confusing or threatening. The rules for safety and survival can be rigid and severe, whether those rules are imposed by the laws of nature or by ideologies and institutions. So our focus tends to be limited to the immediate situations in which we find ourselves, our scope of attention is restricted, and we strive for stability, perhaps even survival.

This perspective has some of the characteristics of early childhood, even though adults regularly experience it. In addition to stability and survival values, the Grounding perspective also encompasses childlike curiosity, simple affection, and a sense of wonder and awe, and for adults these values may become the roots of a renewed life perspective even though its experience may have been triggered through crisis. In times of crisis and prolonged stress, the values in this perspective are those on which we depend as a first step in returning to a more stable, secure reality.[57] It is also quite possible that people can identify a Grounding core perspective because they are associated with someone, or some group, whose Grounding needs are not being met, and so this perspective can become important by association.

Values typical of the Grounding Perspective are:

Affection, Curiosity, Food and Shelter, Kindness, Obedience, Physical Functioning, Maintenance, Safety, Self-Restraint, Sensuality, and Wonder.

Grounding Perspective Example

(All examples in this book are based on actual situations, and our own experiences and observations. We have significantly changed identifying details, and of course the names of people involved.)

Linda was a very intelligent, articulate, healthy, and energetic person. As a young professional woman working as an executive assistant in a financial institution, it was surprising that she had a primary core perspective in Grounding, which would usually be operating as a quiet foundation for most people with that description, and who generally have been accustomed to being able to fulfill very basic needs as a matter of course. Values she had selected on the Values Perspective survey, such as self-confidence, responsibility and competence, suggested that a lot of her energy was in the Management perspective. As we talked to her, however, we learned she was a new mom. It can be difficult enough for new parents to find their footing. Added to this, however, Linda's aging mother had a stroke, and her father was incapable of managing her care on his own. Like many people whose circumstances are demanding a re-valuing that necessitates consciously activating Grounding perspective values, like physical functioning, she was feeling significant anxiety

57 This concept, termed locus of control, was described by Julian B. Rotter in 1966. Rotter classified *internals*, who attribute events to their own control, and *externals*, who attribute events in their life to external circumstances.

about how she would handle what was going to be required of her in the very near future.

When we asked her about her values, she said that responsibility was important for her. Competence was also a key value for Linda, one that she felt strongly defined who she was. Her value of self-confidence was now being called into question by her unaccustomed feelings of uncertainty about what to do, and whether she was doing the right things. As we talked, it seemed clearer to Linda that it should be natural to feel that these values were being challenged because of the burgeoning and unaccustomed demands being placed on her as she tried to maintain equilibrium. She also recognized that under her present circumstances, it had begun to be increasingly difficult to feel 'like herself,' and that she could take steps to take care for her own energy. She had selected the value of physical functioning as a very high priority because of her concerns for her baby and her parents, but on reflection acknowledged that this might also be a key value to take into consideration for herself, by making sure she could continue to exercise regularly, which up to now had always helped her to relax and to maintain a sense that she could be physically competent to meet the demands in her life.

Linda saw that she had a tendency to see the entire responsibility of her parents falling on her alone. Recognizing this, and the need to re-energize herself by feeling increased competence to handle her situation, she resolved to ask for more help of her husband and her other relatives than she might otherwise have done, letting them know what her needs might be at any given moment, and specific ways they could help her. She also decided to avail herself of an elder-care counseling program that would help her to find advice and resources and to ask her husband to actively partner with her in that. She also decided to look for a counselor or therapist whom she could turn to when the going got rough. Life was going to be difficult for a while, but Linda was now seeing that the Grounding perspective would require her to direct energy toward securing a sufficiently stable plan for managing the most basic needs of those depending on her so that she could turn some of her attention and energy toward other demands in her life. When she has successfully redefined her Grounding perspective values such that she can feel secure in her life choices, Linda is likely to gradually return her focus of energy to her 'native' Management perspective. However, her values foundation will be stronger (we discuss Foundation values below).

Family Perspective

The Family Perspective is marked by one's identification with a primary group. For most of us, the first group we depend upon for direction and structure is family. As we get older, this is usually augmented or replaced by work or social groups that function for us in a similar way. When we are young, it is within this framework each person learns the basic essentials of maintaining relationships with others and begins to exercise responsibility for his or her daily actions. Later in life, many people continue to select their priorities from the Family perspective, which marks the importance of basic individual values like self-worth and which is conditioned by affiliation and interaction values like courtesy, loyalty, and respect. Since many of these values are acquired from an early age, we may become so comfortable with them that we may not be aware of their importance, similarly to how Grounding values can operate. But these Family values begin to inform the basics of our identity within groups, and since many work environments function through group performance, these values can often be highly visible, particularly if they are high priorities that are not being supported with actual behaviors. That is, if people do not have the skills for showing kindness, or respect, for example. Indeed, since we acquire many of these values at the same time we are forming our individual personalities, we are often quite sensitive about the support of many of the values in this perspective because if we perceive a question or challenge regarding values in this perspective, real or not, we may interpret that challenge as a personal threat to our basic identity. All of our values are personal, but it seems that those in the Family Perspective are particularly so. Perhaps, that is because we are often aware of our personal histories, no matter whether those histories are positive or negative.

There are many organizations that successfully operate on a model that has strong family characteristics—for example, valuing loyalty and committing a large percentage of resources to looking after the welfare of one's "own"—even though no real family ties are involved. For small companies, in particular entrepreneurial start-ups, this can be a highly effective way of operating; indeed many successful small companies are family owned, and are run like a family. In large companies, a sense of belonging fostered by generous benefits and family-friendly programs can be a strong factor in attracting and retaining loyal employees, although larger organizations often face challenges when trying to maintain a sense of family closeness when they grow.

In even larger organizations, like the armed services, it has become common in the news to hear interviews with soldiers who re-enlist in the middle of a war to hear them say, "I am going back for my buddies, it's about being with them." Their rationale is not ideological or political; it is clearly about people who are considered to be family. We might begin to assume that focus on the Family perspective would give us enough information to start making predictions about an individual's behavior, but we should be quick to remember that same person may also have priority values from any other perspective, and unless we know a little more, we would be wise withhold such a temptation.

Values typical of the Family Perspective are:

Belief, Belonging, Caretaking, Discipline, Duty, Economic Security, Fairness, Honesty, Legacy, Loyalty, Patience, Playfulness, Recognition, Respect, Self Sacrifice, Self-Worth, Stability, and Tradition.

Family Perspective Example

Tom was the project manager of a large (multi-million dollar) project, a joint venture with a foreign partner. The project was about half way through its projected three-year span and was not going well. In fact, he was the second project manager for this job, the first having been replaced because he could not meet the required deadlines. Tom had excellent analytical and logistical skills, but seemed to be at a standstill in regard to getting the project back on track. The stakes were very high, and the pressure he was feeling from his superiors to show positive results was enormous. The pressure showed in his behavior at work and at home and his reputation for being a "difficult" manager was widespread; he could, and easily did lose his temper at his subordinates. Of course, he knew both the job and his relationships were headed in the same general direction and that this was not good news, but he had no awareness of his own values and style, much less did he have tools with which he could work differently.

Tom was selected as a participant in a leadership program in the hopes he would learn something that could help, and there was plenty of feedback from numerous instruments to help that occur. He was not pleased about having to leave the job for this event. Tom had a Family core perspective, which is associated with a style of leadership that necessarily places the individual at the center of group interactions, which makes that person the principle information gatekeeper and decision maker. Tom expressed this style in terms of his position. In other words, his expectation was to be the sole authority and that resources would be allocated and all personnel mobilized by his fiat. This style of leadership is common and can be quite effective in the appropriate contexts. However, Tom was often autocratic, even dictatorial, and his staff did not trust him because they saw him as being governed by his anger, which was quite obvious to them whenever they experienced his frequent outbursts.

One day, at one of the leadership program sessions, Tom went through a small exercise intended to teach the basics of a developmental interview, using questions to elicit employees' motivations and strengths. Previous to this, such an approach, much less conducting a developmental interview, was simply not a consideration for him. But something clicked for him that day, and he told his coach, "Now I know what to say." When he got back to the job, he put together a binder full of both professional and personal information on each person on his team. Then, he shared it with them. As he held his interviews, he used the binders to show respect toward his team, to indicate he was taking care of each one of them, and was being honest about it. He triggered more than half a dozen Family values, such as courtesy, respect, and loyalty. In about three weeks, his coach (which was one of us) began to get phone calls, and hear stories, "What did you do to Tom? He's a different guy." And the job began to improve a great deal. We wish we could say the company made a lot of money on that job. Part of his responsibility when given the job of taking over was to reduce the ultimate amount of loss. But Tom was able to change things dramatically while he was there, and the lessons he learned, he took with him, applying them in a different situation that wasn't already problematic. His core perspective likely remained the same, but the difference came about because he had shifted his priority values within that perspective, which had helped him to behave quite differently.

This example brings up leadership styles, which is a topic directly related to the values perspectives. There are four basic leadership styles that can be inferred from these values perspectives. We will discuss each of these styles following discussions and examples of the perspectives.

Management Perspective

The Management Perspective is characterized by values typical of successful institutions and organizations. The viewpoint of this perspective is naturally linked to its neighbor, the Family perspective, which contains the values that are as important for working in groups as they are for families and all close relational affinities that are concerned with sharing material resources of any kind. To the extent that organizations and institutions are simply "groups of groups," the values that govern what is important in the Management perspective are more oriented toward managing the priorities in expanded organizational situations rather than being limited to a smaller group. At the same time, though this perspective emphasizes managing and responsibility in general, it does not require anyone to actually be a member of an organization in order to hold and operationalize these values.

Management perspective values are concerned with the source of control for resources and access to positions of authority. From this perspective, the organization or institution is seen as the source of power and authority. Legitimate authority is distributed to various people and typically follows a hierarchy, which also codifies levels of responsibility. Responsibility is held individually, based on technical competence, willingness to assume it, and readiness as assessed by those in higher authority. This is the perspective that most medium sized and larger organizations and corporations would be expected to have established as a core perspective, given that these entities need to rely on many hands working within efficient structures to achieve financial success; and given that they must also satisfy regulatory and financial reporting requirements that are required by larger entities with legally mandated authority.

The first three perspectives, Grounding, Family, and Management, all strive to establish a stable, reliable, and manageable world. Given the pace of global information networks and rapid change, this is a continual challenge. As we look at the three perspectives together, we can see that at an individual level, one's focus, i.e., the span or scope of our attention, begins to widen in conjunction with the change from Grounding to Family to Management. However, in all three, the locus of control, the sense of origin ascribed to what controls our world, is understood to be external to the person. So the individual, in all three of these perspectives, looks to a source outside of him or herself for an ultimate authority, behavioral norms, and perhaps, even for specific answers to problems and questions.

Values typical of the Management Perspective are:

Achievement, Authority, Charity, Competence, Competition, Decisiveness, Efficiency, Financial Success, Hierarchal Ability, Informing, Managing, Order, Patriotism, Predictability, Problem Solving, Productivity, Quality, Recreation, Responsibility, Rule of Law, and Self-Confidence.

Management Perspective Example

Mary is a member of a team that runs a not-for-profit organization working with the public and with government. Mary's boss, Gary, is charismatic and dynamic and his small, hand-picked team supports him in his role as the public face of the organization. The organization is young, and the team is newly formed. Gary knows that team-building is essential, especially given that he travels extensively, and is often away from the team for extended periods of time. The non-profit is housed under the auspices of a university and draws on the university for research and other resources such as its access to grants. In a team retreat, the Values Perspective survey provided a picture, in aggregate, of the team's values. An aggregate report of individual values gave the group some interesting things to discuss. Energy in the Grounding perspective, somewhat unusual for a professional team, revealed that the team has been struggling through the stresses and uncertainties of moving into a new office and that newly-hired members were trying to find their way through the practical challenges as they got their feet on the ground. A large amount of energy was also concentrated in the Expansion perspective. These are idealists, working for a cause, and most of them are relatively young in age, at a time in life where, for many people, idealism has not yet been tempered by the rigors of the world of work and exigencies of hard-ball negotiation. Most of the team individually holds the Relational perspective and trust is an important value for them. However, virtually no energy appeared in the Management perspective. Mary is the only person on the team who holds that perspective. The team knows they need the Managerial perspective, but with so few of those values activated within the team, where will they get it?

Many times, if only one person on the team holds a particular values perspective, the team relies on that person to bring that perspective to the table, which can be exhausting. This is especially true when the rest of the team is not individually investing value in that perspective. This may be the case in spite of the fact that, if you ask them, they acknowledge that they indeed need it. So, far too often their energy tends to be directed elsewhere when that lone member, Mary, needs them to be efficient, and needs to know that order and stability are such that when deadlines impinge against their small team, which they do constantly, everyone is on board and accountable. Such is the case with Mary, who feels she has to push to get people moving in timely fashion, especially since they rely on the strongly hierarchal Management culture of the university, where needed go-aheads often have to come down a chain of command and can take time. One of her top values is achievement, and in coaching, she said of herself, "I never let a ball hit the ground."

Mary also acknowledged that she feels herself to be less flexible than others on the team, especially her boss, Gary. When asked, she said that she is thrown into a state of confusion and emotional imbalance when asked to change things at the last moment, which is frequently the case. She also realized that, in staff meetings, when she knows something will not work, she challenges it without preamble. It happens that Mary comes from a business background and was highly successful in the for-profit milieu, so it puzzled her that her teammates were hard to convince and seemed to take her challenges personally. Mary was at a loss, feeling something rare in her life up until then, inadequacy. "What do I do?"

Mary's energy is strongly Managerial, the team needs it, and being older and more experienced, she is a very valuable team asset. Attempting a big change to try to "fit in" with her team would take a great deal of energy, probably would never work anyway, and would not serve the team. So, how to bring them toward her without sacrificing her Managerial strengths?

In coaching, we came up with two relatively simple solutions to the problem. One, to take the small amount of extra time to verbally ease herself in amongst her Relational peers when she is about to say something she knows from experience they might otherwise resist, consciously adopting the value of being present that her peers hold. The second is simply to find ways to express her energetic requirements. It is likely difficult for her Relational perspective boss, Gary, to understand why changing things quickly creates such disequilibrium for Mary. But, he is also likely to be drawn by his own perspective toward listening, if Mary puts her needs into carefully-chosen words. Mary is articulate, self-aware, extraverted, and determined to use her own value of Achievement to cultivate behaviors that will make it easier for her teammates and boss to value the critically-needed Management view she brings to the table.

Relational Perspective

The Relational perspective deals with a viewpoint that emphasizes degrees or levels of awareness of one's self and one's relationships with others. This viewpoint leads to the development of values directed toward describing and developing self-potential on the one hand, (through values like Balance, Courage, Reflection, and Search-For-Meaning), and for forming and maintaining relationships on the other (though values like Empathy, Diversity, Listening, Openness, and Trust).

The Relational perspective can be understood to contrast with the previous three perspectives in several important ways. First, where the Grounding, Family, and Management perspectives invoke values that support a stable and predictable world, the Relational perspective begins to engage the individual in a more dynamic reality, the changing world of relationships.

Another significant characteristic of this perspective is that the individual assumes control for his or her self, as well as responsibility for his or her decisions and actions. In other words, the locus of control shifts to an internal origin. Values characteristic of this perspective support self-development, effective relationships, and creative work. Effective use of authority in this stage is characterized by facilitative use of listening, asking questions to ensure mutual understanding, and being fully present with others.

This perspective is also notable in that it contains values that are well recognized by individuals and organizations alike as being essential to being generally successful in life, and yet we have observed in our work that the values in this perspective are often selected as aspirations, that is, values which are of a high priority, but for which behavioral skills have not yet been developed or fully developed. And in personal and professional contexts, the lack of relational skills can easily be critically limiting to personal life and career alike.

One more additional note is that the developmental stage models including Fowler, Hall, and Barrett all identify a potential sense of anxiety or even difficulty when an individual moves into this perspective, likely because of both the shift in locus of control, and also due to a cultural lack of relationship skills training that should begin in early life and continue through adolescence, but does not happen, in general. The Relational perspective also contains values that promote change and dynamic activity. With the increase in technologically connected relationships that occur though social media platforms, it remains to be seen if this cultural lack is filled with a new set of skills or whether, to the contrary, a lack of skills will be felt even more keenly.

It is our experience that Relational values are essential for development and directly support values that are found in other perspectives, but they are those that are most often neglected or only given lip-service in many personal and organizational contexts. In many cultures the behaviors that support these values are not often directly supported with behavioral skills training, or even mentioned. We all seem to simply assume that many of these are so self-evidently important that we all just have the competencies to support them, almost as if by magic. However, our experience has shown the opposite to be the case. And the lack of Relational values supporting skills is a major problem for personal and professional development.

VALUES TYPICAL OF THE RELATIONAL PERSPECTIVE ARE:
Acceptance, Analogy, Balance, Being Present, Choice, Commitment, Courage, Creativity, Empathy, Independence, Intimacy, Learning, Listening, Openness, Personal Growth, Questioning, Reflection, Risk, Search For Meaning, Trust, and Well-Being.

RELATIONAL PERSPECTIVE EXAMPLE

One morning at the opening of a routine coaching call, Dave's (the coachee) answer to the question, "How was your weekend?" was a surprising, "Not so good. I had to work all weekend long, so I'm tired." We won't go through all the detail of the weekend. The coachee was the COO of a construction company with a regional presence, managing a $100 million operation. When asked for specifics, he said that a problem with an important job had surfaced at the last minute on the Friday before, and an inspection was scheduled for that Monday. The COO would normally not have been involved with on-the-ground problem solving. But in this case, he had to step in and set things right. This involved invoking resources, personnel and equipment, which represented a cost overrun, but solving the problem was critical to avoid even more expensive penalties if the inspection date was not met and passed.

"At least a couple of weeks," was Dave's response when asked "About how much earlier do you think the problem actually became known to the project manager?" And then after his response, the follow up bomb of a question, "Why do you think he didn't call you earlier?" After some discussion, it became apparent that the project manager was fairly young and was afraid that Dave would blame him personally for the problem, so he spent the two weeks trying to solve it on his own and only called Dave in at the last minute when all else had failed.

The underlying problem though was that Dave had a reputation for being extremely demanding of success and aggressively punishing of failure. He was known for excellence, but at the price of relational trust. No one dared to go to him and say, "I have a problem—can I get your advice?" They knew that they would be called on the carpet and be publicly "reamed a new one." We didn't have to go through the numbers to show Dave how much his lack of relational skills had just cost. It was obvious. And so was his frustration when he realized that he was going to have to change some very old habits and change his priorities if he ever expected people to trust him with problems, not just with successful answers. And to be fair to Dave, the problem was larger than his own behavior. The entire organization had a "sink or swim" mentality where younger project managers were placed in the field and were given little support and almost no mentoring. So while the company had a reputation for professional excellence and personal responsibility, the uncounted cost remained extremely high.

Dave's insight in the wake of this event and others he could remember that were too much like it to ignore, was that he needed to give greater priority to Relational perspective values. He needed, in simple terms, to value the practical effects of cultivating relationships. In his case, this would require two changes. One would be to make the effort to re-prioritize his value of excellence, making a trade-off that gave listening a higher priority, and seeking some basic listening skills. Listening is a Relational value. It means that we are prepared, at least temporarily, but nevertheless genuinely, to set aside whatever agenda we may have in order to take in what another person is saying, and consider their information and their viewpoint with both respect and objectivity. This would not require that he cease to value quality as a priority for the company; rather, that he would need to figure out how to keep the quality message front-and-center, while at the same time make sure that his people got the message that, although they were expected to do a quality job, they were not out there on their own. The second, more long-term, change would be to go about making sure that his own reports be made aware of the consequences of failing to listen, and to hold them accountable to making it possible for problems to be shifted upwards in the chain of command before the problems hurt the company. He would have to listen to them, too.

Dave was a Managerial perspective leader, who valued whatever he could quantify for the good of the company balance-sheet. In coming to the conclusion that he needed to more highly prioritize people-oriented, Relational values, he became determined to extend his values reach in order to achieve real, "on-the-ground" excellence as a Manager.

Systems Perspective

The Systems perspective is concerned with the big picture. It invokes values that place a priority on being able to keep track of an entire system or systems and invokes interdependence as a primary value. This is a perspective where the focus of attention is constantly in motion, as well as the relationships that create and hold the system together. With a Systems core perspective, one is aware that the world is dynamic, and constantly in motion. A quick look at the individual who holds this as a core perspective will show that person is aware that he or she simply cannot keep track of and manage everything alone. The systems person is one who knows he or she needs others, and often, the goals and objectives those people share are of a much more broad scope than any of the previously discussed perspectives. This perspective necessarily deals with relationships, and involves others in collaborative and mutually accountable ways, so the use of authority, particularly in organizations, is often characterized by an attitude of temporary stewardship rather than the sense of singular responsibility that is characteristic of other perspectives. By definition, this perspective represents a worldview that fully accepts integrity, ethics, and partnership as keys to successful development and achievement.

There are some immediate challenges presented to a person or group whose core perspective is Systems. Perhaps, the most obvious is the challenge of communication with people whose core or focus is in the Family or Management perspectives, and who hold a very different world view. It is very easy to lose sight of the importance of maintaining strong, active skills associated with values found in the Family and Management views. Additionally, much of the time the values in this perspective are a part of our vision values cluster, which means they are more aspirational than operational ; thus, likely to lack behavioral skills to support them. This should not be understood as a criticism in any way. But this characteristic can be, at the same time, a strength (provides vision) and a weakness (behavioral skills necessary to bring the vision into reality may be lacking).

This perspective also carries with it additional responsibilities to possess and practice effective communication skills with people from all other perspectives. One of the limitations we have regularly observed of people with a Systems core perspective is that they may simply lack awareness of the priorities of other perspectives. They may lack the ability to understand the priorities of other perspectives, through simply failing to value them. Remedying this may not be an easy adjustment, but it is accomplished by mastering some of the key values and skill sets in the Relational Awareness perspective, especially Listening, Questioning, and Openness.

Values typical of the Systems Perspective are:
Beauty, Collaboration, Community, Development, Dialogue, Empowering Others, Equality, Exploration, Flexibility, Innovation, Integrity, Interdependence, Intuition, Partnership, Service, Simultaneity, Strategy, and Sustainability.

Systems Perspective Example

Al is the director of a large health care organization. He had brought us in to work with a group of physicians in one of the clinical practice groups under his management and set the brief for the workshop we were to deliver. He sat in on the workshop, and his presence, far from being inhibiting—as can sometimes be the case when a superior is present—was not only acceptable, but clearly comfortable for the team members. He was not only well respected, but was individually felt to be on good terms with everyone in the team.

The immediate problem was that the group was not bringing in the funding they once did, and their rating had begun to slip from being recognized as one of the top ten departments in the nation. The deterioration had begun to affect their ability to attract the top percentile of new doctors to the team. Each physician was absolutely top-notch in his or her individual practice. But Al recognized that getting the group back to their highest-level excellence rating depended on what kind of environment they were able to create for incoming professionals and interns, for the professions that reported to the team, and for the team members themselves to operate in harmony in such a way that the 'intangibles' could be felt by everyone involved in a positive and engaging way. In medicine, the physicians are the experts who make the decisions that affect the priorities and processes followed by every staff member. Al also recognized that the doctors needed to cultivate an atmosphere in which their individual authority was unquestioned while also making room for staff to be able to be secure in their own competence to carry out instructions from peer physicians on the team and their legitimate proxies at any given time without feeling that unspoken, but nevertheless emotionally perceivable turf boundaries might be violated, with possible consequences to peer doctors, staff or, of course, their patients. Al is a Systems perspective manager who understood the value of such subtle interdependence and how community of purpose is created very often through implicit and at times non-verbal cues. He recognized that there were unspoken conflicts between some of the team members, and that although the conflicts were not openly acknowledged or alluded to, newer members of the team were already withdrawing emotionally, preferring to concentrate on their own work.

During the kickoff team workshop, we asked team members to share a personal story about a formative experience. People told remarkable stories, some about past professional situations and some about personal situations. All of the stories were offered sincerely for the learning benefit of all. Al shared his story close to the end of the exercise. He talked how he had created a situation that required a sizeable commitment in software development, and to be successful, also required the collaboration of several other companies that would normally be thought of as "the competition." But the project, if successful, would be a win-win for everyone, even the governmental regulation agency involved.

The project was all going well, but at the last minute, one of the other companies pulled its support out. Suddenly, almost all the other players withdrew or at least put their previous commitments on hold, leaving Al with a very large financial commitment at risk should the project fail. But Al had done his homework, and knew that his original idea was sound. He told no one because at that moment, it would have only ensured disaster. In the end he was able to pull off the deal. Al had brought to bear his Systems values of strategy, risk, and research. But he recognized, and admitted that, though his aspiration was collaboration and the project depended on it, he had failed to make the effort required to adequately communicate, and ensure complete mutual understanding and agreement with people who did not share his same perspective, in terms they would both understand and value early enough to ensure everyone was really on the same page. He learned, he said, that he had made the mistake of making assumptions that other people would understand his perspective without extra effort on his part, when in fact they did not.

The room went silent as Al told his story, and people realized that their own futures would have been dramatically impacted by the failure of this project. Of course, it succeeded, and everyone knew that because they were all still sitting around the same table. But the amazement was palpable.

Al did not attend the subsequent team workshop sessions, leaving the team to continue on its own. But his candid story made a point that the physician team took to heart in their subsequent meetings. As peers, they had shared personal stories in good faith. It still made an impact that their own manager was willing to empower others, not only with his example, but also through his choosing to support the group's candidness by meeting it with his own willingness to be vulnerable, sharing information that was not previously known, in the interest of community building. In the course of their workshop sessions, the physician team continued to exchange sometimes sensitive and personal information that they had not done previously because of felt injunctions against sharing anything that might cause their professionalism to be questioned in the minds of their peers. Instead, they eventually agreed upon a shared set of values that they would hold themselves mutually accountable to, which included ensuring mutual understanding, taking into account differing values perspectives held amongst themselves, and by the other professionals they depended on so that their patients would be served with competence, efficiency and caring. A year later, they showed us that they were still using the same list of values, and revisited it at every team meeting, to make sure they were still acting in accordance with their values, with their support professionals, their patients, and with each other.

Expansion Perspective

The Expansion Perspective values work with the largest scope and application of values we can access. These are always aspirational values, representing energy that pulls us toward a vision of global effects and proportions. As such they are less likely to be completely supported by necessary and associated skills and competencies. While these values act as guides to our progress and development, it does not mean we cannot at least partially achieve what these values represent in terms of accomplishments. This perspective includes the values we most often associate with singular historical and legendary personalities, saints and statesmen whom we revere as examples.

However, do not be deceived into thinking that only saints and great leaders can operate in this perspective. As we write this, the issue of global climate change has begun to create an awareness and sensitivity that is seated in this perspective; millions of "ordinary" people are beginning to appreciate values in this orientation. Their awareness is truly expanding to include a concern for the health of the Earth. In fact, nearly any issue can be understood in terms of its potential impact on a global scale. A daily glance at movements in the stock market when considering the current political and cultural crises will reaffirm that claim, and make the argument for the importance of this perspective being available to anyone and everyone.

This perspective represents a worldview that is always great in terms of scope, for awareness from this view can include the entire planet. The perspective presented here is one that nearly cycles back to the Grounding Perspective, in the sense that the Expansion Perspective recognizes that the scope encompassed is so great that one cannot ever be in control, nor can one assume individual responsibility for implementing these values on a global or national level. Values in this perspective, for the most part, require the mutual support of others for whom these values are also a high priority.

Global climate change is now an established reality. The consideration of this current situation challenges us to expand our awareness just by its very nature. At this writing, we notice two representative responses to this issue. The first is that once people have become aware of the issue, they are faced with the challenge of what to do that is significant and seems worthy of the issue. Frustration can be the result of not understanding the nature of working with values in this perspective, given that its scope far exceeds the individual grasp and requires active participation in highly interdependent, yet dynamic and widely dispersed global networks. The second thing we notice is that, while most people cannot actually apply the concept of global climate change at a global level, they may be sufficiently energized by the value of planetary ecology to envision means to ground it in their own or another specific location or region. That is, their personal vision is not of great enough scope to be engaged in the concept at a global level, but they can and do engage, as the nature of their own expansiveness will allow. This does not keep them from exercising values in this perspective.

It should be remembered that, no matter what their core perspective may be, anyone can select values that span the complete scope of the perspectives described above, regardless of focus, or a person may limit his or her selections to operate from within certain viewpoints. Whether one's span is broad or more circumscribed, each sort of profile presents advantages and strengths as well as challenges and limitations.

Values typical of the Expansion Perspective are:

Altruism, Detachment, Global Enfranchisement, Human Rights, Inspiring Others, Mind-Body Integration, Nonviolence, Planetary Ecology, Reconciliation, Simplification, and Spirituality.

Expansion Perspective Example

Marian is a recruiter for one of the larger non-governmental organizations, and a lengthy values conversation with her was extremely helpful to our understanding of what the Expansion perspective can look like "on the ground." She enlists people with the myriad skills needed to go into a part of the world where population displacement is taking place due to natural calamities, such as typhoon or tsunami, or in certain cases, in which populations are at risk of starvation or disease due to displacement as a result of political unrest. Her life is dedicated to serving humanity.

When disaster strikes, she typically draws on a population scattered around the globe of people with relevant skills and experience like triage medicine, engineering, and water management. Her view is of necessity a global perspective, as she works with individuals and partner NGOs and other organizations whose reach is worldwide. Often, these entities are drawing on the same pool of dedicated first-responders and must find ways to cooperate in sharing people and financial resources. Too, she and her counterparts in other organizations have become well aware that the first-responder pool must be recruited and developed, sustained, and released when burn-out occurs, a phenomenon now well-recognized and acknowledged by the global first-responder community. In doing what she does, she draws too on Systems perspective values like collaboration and development, as well as Relational perspective values like listening and openness. Management perspective values are essential to her role, including competence, efficiency, informing, problem solving, and notably, rule of law. So are Family perspective values such as patience and respect.

In this book, we have emphasized the limitations of stage models with their inherent "more is better" bias and implicit linearity. We have arranged our perspectives in a circle, which we nevertheless acknowledge derives from the stage-model. However, we have observed a paradoxical linkage between what is usually the "lowest" stage in the traditional models, and the "highest." The folk wisdom of cultures worldwide recognizes that a fool may look like a sage, and vice-versa, to the extent that it can be hard to tell them apart. The global first-responder community is an excellent example of what many of our myths tell us, which is that Grounding and Expansion share some of the same characteristics, and that representing the values perspectives as a complete circle (in fact, it looks more like a spiral, but more about that later) has a justification in how values play out in real life.

The survival values of the Grounding perspective cannot be ignored. We all need to eat and be able to provide shelter for our children. The person who has to be consciously concerned with this perspective on a daily basis may be pitied, but may also be seen as having too narrow a focus, perhaps not so different from a fool, particularly when those around him or her may not need to be concerned with survival and instead whose attention is focused toward the kinds of daily activities that are more highly valued in more "developed" societies. The people whose perspective is for whatever reason Grounding, may be shunned, and may also be seen as a political liability, particularly when intervening to provide for their needs may come at a cost of resource and energy from people whose focus is elsewhere.

The sage, of course, is often seen as neglecting exactly the same values that occupy the focus of society at large. The reason may be different, for example, a high degree of spirituality, leading the sage into a state of detachment from worldly goods, social appearances, and the more traditional relational ties of kinship and family of origin affiliations. The view is Expansion, and the sage sees from a global perspective that, because it is so broad, requires distance.

The first-responder who is deployed by a global NGO of the kind that Marian works for, lands on the ground, often in unfamiliar or unsecured territory (for example, after-shocks of an earthquake may still be occurring). Water, shelter, food and security are the first things the individual first-responder needs to secure, before turning to the problems that need solving in the immediate vicinity. Grounding values are triggered first, by absolute necessity and by fiat. Only then are that individual's focus values, which drove him to attain the skills and expertise he brings, brought into play. All the time, he will be well aware that a global organization, the workings of which may remain largely invisible due to their extent, and in this respect resembling a global web of relationships and interactions, which includes Marian, is making his efforts on the ground possible. He would not be here otherwise. Idealism put into practice to this degree may look like stark foolishness to the rest of the world, no matter how much they may nevertheless be grateful that these people are doing a job that very few could possibly envision.

"Validating" Values and Perspectives.

When working with values, it is always imperative to avoid classifying or stereotyping oneself or others with regard to the values perspectives (and we caution values practitioners to prevent clients from doing so). A person having a core in *any* perspective can live a productive and satisfying life. We have seen many people whose Focus is in the Grounding or Expansion perspective operating in completely functional and healthy ways. It should be remembered that it is up to each person to 'validate' his or her own values priorities and perspectives. That is, to ask themselves what their values mean to them, how they uniquely define their values, and how they operate in their lives; and, if, for example, when looking at the values they have chosen through the survey process, they find the fit is insufficient, to determine for themselves (and a coach can be very helpful here) what values *are* important to them and why.

Leadership Styles Driven By Values

We have worked extensively in the field of leadership development, and have extensively applied the Values Perspective theory in our work. The concept of leadership is recognized for its importance, and receives a great deal of attention from theorists and researchers; yet at the same time, it has remained elusive and difficult to describe succinctly. Part of the problem is a lack of agreement on what constitutes an effective leader, or even what "leadership" is. For us, leadership is fundamentally a function of a relationship between leader and follower or supporter. A leader is one who exerts influence on those that support him or her. There are many potential opportunities for the exercise of leadership, and only some of them require some sort of designated authority. But, every instance of the exercise of leadership involves the question of values because when one undertakes to influence another, that influence necessarily invokes the question of priorities and resultant behaviors, which as we have just discussed are, at the most basic levels, driven at least in part, by values.

As we have worked with both values theory and assessment, and put those in the context of leadership development, we began to see the patterns of four basic leadership styles; styles that could be described by the Values Perspective model. We will discuss the connection between values and behavior more thoroughly below, but for now it is important to point out that values are tied directly to behavior, but that a single value can drive multiple behaviors. This principle can be generalized to leadership in saying that these styles can be concluded or inferred from the perspectives just previously discussed, and at the same time, one is not confined to any particular leadership style, no matter what values one identifies with or what perspective is most natural to a person.

These four styles are Individual-Centered, Designated Authority, Relational, and Systems leadership. In our paper, "Values Driven Leadership," we discuss these styles in detail, compare and contrast them to current leadership theory, and provide historical and current examples of them.[58] What follows is a summary of those styles with some discussion regarding the strengths and limitations of each.

In the past, leadership has usually been described in terms of three general perspectives: The trait model identifies traits of successful leaders with a tacit prescription to emulate, as closely as possible, a chosen model. The functional model focuses on successful processes and procedures that implement the operations or functions of leadership, again with the same tacit prescription of emulation. The situational model is more flexible, and suggests an effective leader shifts along a continuum of prescribed styles ranging from highly directive to highly delegative, depending on the competencies and readiness of those in subordinate positions.[59]

The term "Servant Leadership," first coined by Robert Greenleaf in 1970, defines leadership not by trait or function, but by a set of values that emphasizes listening, humility, service-to-others, and vision.[60]

All of these models have proponents and critics, all of them emphasize certain aspects of leadership. As of yet, there is no single model that captures and explains the complex realities of leadership. The values perspective can show why this continues to be the case in leadership literature, and why a single style of leadership is neither always appropriate nor desired.

Looking at leadership through the lens of values views provides a different and insightful look at this complex subject. We suggest leadership styles do follow the natural flow of changing perceptions across the Values Perspective model. However, we do not suggest a different leadership style for each perspective. To do so would be to lock a given leader into a behavioral set of skills that is confining, and does not represent the behavior of most leaders. These four basic leadership styles can be inferred from the perspectives as previously discussed, as follows:

Grounding	Family	Management	Relational	Systems	Expansion
Individual-Centered Leadership		Designated Authority Leadership	Relational Leadership	Systems Leadership	

Fig. 11 — Four Basic Leadership Styles

58 For a complete discussion of these styles, with comparisons to current leadership theory and examples see Kenton Hyatt and Cheryl De Ciantis, "Values Driven Leadership," Integral Leadership Review (October, 2012), http://integralleadershipreview.com/7601-values-driven-leadership/.

59 Tom D. Daniels and Barry K. Spiker, *Perspectives on Organizational Communication*, 3d. ed. (Madison, WI: Brown & Benchmark Publishers, 1994) 230-235.

60 See Robert K. Greenleaf, *Servant Leadership* (Mahwah, NJ: Paulist Press, 1991). See also Peter Block, *Stewardship*. (San Francisco:Barrett-Koehler Publishers, 1996).

Individual-Centered Leadership

Grounding and Family perspective values are oriented around a single governing concept: Security. The Grounding perspective refers to the basics of survival and maintenance, while the Family perspective refers to the basics of security within a primary social group. This security can be achieved through a variety of means depending on the situation. Since the environments that demand a core in either of the above two perspectives are those in which the physical, psychological and/or social protection is supplied by the leader, attention is placed on the individual leader as the primary means by which anything is organized or accomplished.

This is a fundamentally directive leadership style, which can take many forms. In a child's world, this style is both necessary and welcome. The leader (parent) is the source for security and explanation for the nature of the world. In high stress or emergency situations, a strong directive style is both appropriate and lacking in explanation, since action must be taken according to direction and without question. In groups, the structure of individual-as-center leadership requires a strong gatekeeper role with regard to information and outside relationships, and the leader must approve of all activities and relational links.

This style can be effective and productive in small organizations, but it requires that followers share a similar perspective, and the resulting leadership style is "just the way it is." This leadership style can be described as parental in nature because of its similarity to the role that parents assume with children, especially when they are small and security is of paramount concern, and a child generally wants and expects to be taken care of. We would not want to suggest this is always an appropriate term to use with this leadership style, simply because the powerful connotations (both positive and negative) that "parent" carries with it. Nevertheless, the analogy holds in many respects. Individual-Centered leadership usually marks the style of the entrepreneur, or the inventor who creates and runs a start-up. This leader may be the only person in the business who actually understands the technicalities of what is being produced or created. This is a necessary style, but one that may carry unexpected responsibility for the leader.

Individual-Centered leadership often makes clear those who are considered to be "insiders" or "outsiders." When this perspective and leadership style is generalized to a large social or cultural level, it shows itself through attitudes and behaviors of ethnocentrism, sectarianism, xenophobia, and exceptionalism. Status and prestige is highly important and marked by being a group insider, identified by the display of insider knowledge and by routine behavior and obedience. Gaining favor and personal approval are governing issues for each group member.

In small organizations where the group core perspective is Family, the necessary centrality and directive quality of the leader tends to keep the organizational structure tight, with true delegated authority at a minimum, usually to a few tested individuals. Leader behavior may appear benign, but dependence on the leader does not change. In less than optimum circumstances, the leader may become authoritarian or dictatorial with a punitive, "My way or the highway," style. As a leader's status grows, so does dependence on that person. We call this the "Great Man" style of leadership, where the leader may assume a guru type of position (more often than not in the limited, non-generative sense), involving attribution of personal knowledge and power, control of resources, and being an information gatekeeper.

In larger organizations, for example, many theocratic and some military organizations, questioning of the centrality of the leader is simply not allowed if an individual is to maintain membership in the group. This style also breaks down in a number of ways as the organization grows in scope and complexity. Eventually, the biggest challenge this style presents is that of succession. Even when succession passes to a groomed, literal family member, the new leader must quickly establish credibility that he in fact is capable of filling the prior leader's shoes with regard to the established expectations of organizational members. However, many organizations that start with a "family" model, with a strong central founder and leader, however appropriate that culture may be to the phase of organizational life-cycle in which it was established, have great difficulty in changing to a culture that supports a different leadership style when internal factors like growth and external factors such as global competition make it difficult to sustain.

Some of the benefits of the Individual-Centered leadership style can be seen in operation even in large organizations. Values like loyalty, stability, belonging and economic security can attract employees who return loyalty to the organization, sometimes for generations. In heavy-industrial sectors, for example, where safety and physical security are vital, strong centralized leadership that mandates and maintains regulations can save lives. We have seen the CEO of a four-billion dollar company publicly weep when informed of the death of an employee on the job and put his personal energy into redoubling efforts to ensure safety. His Family perspective values were quite sincere and regarded as such by employees.

This feeling of familial connection resulted in a high degree of retention, even among seasonal workers, who would return to the company by preference over other opportunities.

One note of caution: Individual-Centered leadership is not the same as Charismatic leadership. Charisma is a personal quality based in a variety of traits, which create a magnetic attractiveness for a person. Charisma can be expressed in any perspective, but if a charismatic leader uses that quality to create dependence on his or her self, then he or she would be also using the Individual-Centered leadership style. In such cases, functionally separating the two would be very difficult, if not impossible.

Designated Authority Leadership

Leadership that is primarily defined by designated authority is the quintessential characteristic of hierarchical organizations. The values in the Management perspective are concerned with efficiency and organizational structure. Leadership in large organizations is dependent on the ability of an individual to first establish and then interpret policy and standardized procedure. The shift from the central position of the leader, to the central position of the office of the leader (as established by the delegated authority from the institution), is a fundamental difference from the Individual-Centered leadership style.

This style is the classic, modernistic manager style, often described in the literature as "command and control" leadership, and is found throughout the world in corporate, not-for-profit, educational, and governmental situations. It is based in fundamental assumptions and principles of mechanistic scale and span of control that depend on accountability and responsibility as defined by role. Followers are group members first, requiring a sense of belonging and basic respect, but being dependent on institutional orthodoxy for "the way we do things here," which is as much tacit convention as it is explicit direction. Reward and punishment is much more a function of accountability and problem solving than duty. Loyalty is valued, differing from the Grounding and Family Perspectives, in the respect that it is accorded to the institution and roles defined within it rather than to the individual leader.

The general objective of this leadership style is the establishment and maintenance of a stable environment. Such an environment will allow for maximum efficiency, and eventual predictability in regard to strategic planning. Rationality then, is the primary means for governing. The assumption is that the leader can literally *think* him- or herself to success. Obviously, this leadership style lends itself to the strengths of particular cognitive preferences and styles, and creates a cycle of self-selection, in other words, hiring for the same values, and reinforcing institutional mindsets. Evidence for this phenomenon is well established through various areas of research, but a good example is in the Myers-Briggs Type Indicator research finding that people with a Thinking preference tend to self-select into positions that allow them to leverage this natural tendency.[61]

This is a powerful and productive leadership style that leads to effective critical thinking and the achievement of tangible objectives, assuming that change factors in the internal and external environment can be sufficiently anticipated and managed. Indeed, a subset of this style might legitimately be identified as a management style of leadership, or what is often simply referred to as Management. But while it often includes managing, it is actually much more than that. We suggest that all managers have leadership opportunities and all leaders have management responsibilities.

However, Designated Authority leadership may fall short in exploiting the long-term competitive advantages derived from forming and sustaining positive relationships between leaders and supporters, not to mention customers, since relationship skills tend to be viewed simply as "tools" of effective leaders. It may also lack the agility that derives from flexible structures and attitudes because it depends on the establishment and maintenance of a stable environment, even though in reality, the environment is complex and changing. The advantages of this style can be seen, for example, when predictable outcomes are seen to enhance financial success for selected stakeholders, and when well-ordered and impartial systems of compensation, whether negative or positive, are seen to function impartially, and employees may feel they receive the rewards or otherwise that they expect. In the case of Mary, discussed above, her Management core perspective put her at odds with peers who had not come from Management perspective organizations and who interpreted Mary's competent advice as criticism. She could not understand why her present teammates were unreceptive and even offended, when her previous reports and peers had taken it completely in stride and shared a similar style, viewing it as more efficient, given that the focus was on solving the problem at hand.

---

61 Isabel Briggs Myers et al., *MBTI Manual: A Guide to the Development and Use of the Myers Briggs Type Indicator*, 3d ed. (Palo Alto, CA: Consulting Psychologists Press, Inc. 1989), 10.

Designated Authority is the leadership style for which people are most often rewarded in modern societies (and their organizations), so it should not be surprising that this is the style of leadership most often taught and emulated.

Relational Leadership

A leadership style based on the Relational perspective presents quite a dramatic difference from the Designated Authority style discussed above. The Relational perspective is composed of values that support self and relationship development and maintenance. This awareness presupposes that the dynamics of relationship are a centrally defining characteristic for this leadership style. Interestingly, this dynamic also occurs in a distorted form in the "Great Man" aspect of the Individual-Centered leadership style, as exemplified by values like respect and courtesy, but which are nearly completely directed one-way, and most of the relational energy is aimed toward pleasing the central figure. By contrast, the Relational Leadership style requires self-awareness as well as other awareness. Even more, it assumes that relationship is a fundamental part of existence, and that all of us are in relationships as a given precondition to our existence. Therefore, the first requirement of this style of leadership is to discover one's own style of relating, and then begin to develop the basic skills of connecting to others based on their own perspectives. The Relational Leadership style is far more than simply having more conversations with others, and because people are different, it is a challenging and at times confusing style to work with.

There is a great deal of research regarding the competitive advantages of this leadership style. One recent summary defined leadership style as "the manager's ability to support, encourage, coach, and empower his or her staff so as to facilitate employee self-confidence, self-management, and interpersonal interactions."[62] What tends to be overlooked with regard to the Relational Leadership style is that there are potential barriers to its effectiveness, which we have often seen in organizations of all types and sizes. Four of the most important are:

62 Laird Mealiea and Ramon Baltazar, "A Strategic Guide for Building Effective Teams," *Public Personnel Management* 34, no. 2 (2005), 141ff, accessed August 21, 2013, http://www.questia.com/PM.qst?a=o&d=5012090317.

- Relational Leadership is foreign to current organizational culture, which is capitalistic and competitive rather than relationally cooperative.

- The majority of successful individuals in leadership positions in organizations possess cognitive styles that prioritize rational processes over relational processes.[63]

- Compensation and reward structures are not designed to support a style that may not result in immediately or easily measurable results, especially financial results.

- There is little effective training, especially early in a potential leader's education and career, in regard to the attitudes and skills that would support Relational Leadership.

The point is that when an individual begins to see the world from the Relational perspective, and values a Relational Leadership approach, he or she must be prepared to operate from a position that may enjoy little real external and internal support, no matter how much ink is spent on praising the virtues of this value set. This can be an extremely uncomfortable process to begin, and to sustain long enough to develop skills that can then begin to show tangible results.

A special mention regarding creativity and this leadership style is appropriate. While all people are creative in whatever focus perspective they may enjoy (it's never a matter of *whether* people are creative, just *how* they are creative), the explicit need for innovative creativity (the knack for stepping outside problem definitions), is fostered by the values of the Relational perspective as opposed to adaptive creativity and problem solving (creativity exercised within the parameters of a given problem or context boundaries) which is supported by the values of the Management perspective.[64] Teresa Amabile and Stanley Gryskiewicz describe six organizational factors that account for innovative creativity: freedom to pursue a problem, challenge of the work itself, sufficient resources, group support, manager support, and organizational encouragement.[65] At least

63 Michael M. Lombardo, Robert W. Eichinger and Roger P. Pearman, *You: Being More Effective in Your MBTI Type* (Minneapolis, MN: Lominger, 2005), 5.

64 For a discussion of adaptive versus innovative creativity, see Michael Kirton, *Adaptors and Innovators* (London: Taylor & Francis Books Ltd., 1989). See also http://www.kaicentre.com.

65 Teresa M. Amabile and Stanley S. Gryskiewicz, *Creativity in the R&D Laboratory*, Technical Report No. 30 (Center for Creative Leadership, 1987). For a more extensive

three, and possibly four of these factors, are greatly influenced by the relationships that an individual has with self and others. This is not to say that creativity cannot occur without these factors in place, but that it is greatly enhanced by them as it occurs within organizations, as leaders develop and maintain supporting relationships with others and create environments that foster relationship.

Systems Leadership

The governing concept for this leadership style is valuing an awareness that operating at the level of systems requires interdependent relationships. Often this style of leading is characterized in terms of a wide scope of vision compared with other perspectives, implying that leaders are able to see beyond organizational norms and boundaries. However, while a wider scope may be a function of this leadership style, stressing that characteristic creates a description of this style of leading that misrepresents it.

Leadership at this level includes a visionary, futuristic aspect, and includes both issues and values that are oriented toward what is commonly referred to as the "vision" in regard to an individual or an organization. We will discuss the Vision Cluster of values as a working dynamic in Part IV. Because of this, a Systems Leadership perspective and style immediately challenges a leader to be able to communicate and relate to others who do not share this perspective, and who may have a far different understanding of the values represented in the Systems and Expansion Perspectives, which support this leadership style. We commonly encounter people in positions that have been required to shift their leadership style from a Management perspective, which supports a Designated Authority Leadership style, to the Systems perspective, which supports a Systems Leadership style, without the necessary support of Relational Leadership skills. This can result in an ambiguous situation where the leader is feeling the pull of a "comfort zone" style that depends on authority and direct management when lacking an understanding of how to manage from a Systems perspective, which requires relationship skills because a system is not defined by its objective parts, but by its interactions and relationships.

Over a number of years, we have worked with a series of cohorts in a Sustainable Management graduate degree program, of which there

---

discussion see Teresa M. Amabile, *Creativity in Context* (Boulder, CO: Westview Press, 1996).

are many, administering the Values Perspective survey and presenting the aggregated results for the students to discuss. A Systems perspective value, Sustainability, always appeared near the top of every cohort's list of highest-priority values at the group level. Interestingly, when asked, the groups were unable to offer their definition of the term. It appeared that they might have a tacit expectation of what it meant, but only a few individuals had actually spent any time reflecting on it. Groups may reveal as much by what they fail to select as important as what they do prioritize. In this case, a few values always appeared at the bottom of the complete values list (meaning that no or very few individuals selected it when given the opportunity in the course of the survey). It might be assumed that the value of Tradition would hold little energy for relatively young people (in this case, already working) educating themselves for advancement in a leading-edge field. In the U.S., the value of Patriotism may be understood by many as a code-word to express an over-determined political bias, therefore, undesirable or irrelevant (and likely a negative code-word, which when rejected may denote forward-thinking). However, two additional values were least important to these cohorts: Hierarchal Ability and Rule of Law. Our challenge to them was, "What will be your message, as an agent for change, advocating for sustainability, either internally or externally, to large organizations whose leadership may not value the Systems perspective?" Failing to place value on hierarchal ability could mean that a message is aimed toward an audience without the power to act upon it; or that the nature of hierarchy itself, which is foundational to Designated Authority leadership and the Management perspective held by many organizations (and not only for-profit organizations) may be unintentionally critiqued and those who value it alienated — or, the message may simply not connect. A greater blind-spot, in our view, is failing to value rule of law, when it is precisely both enlightened and well-founded regulatory structure that will be necessary to implement sustainability initiatives at any appreciable scale.

We have found that a great challenge for people with a Systems perspective, who are in or aspiring to leadership positions, is to "value" more foundational concepts — and the people who hold them. Community and Collaboration are both Systems perspective values, and both concepts require the more-foundational Management and Relational perspective values to be in place. For many people who value a Systems leadership approach, these values and skills are not necessarily in place. This is why we believe Systems leadership, and representative values such as collaboration, are not so easy to attain, and for this reason are at the true, growing edge of leadership development.

A Systems approach to leadership must include the values of the individual leader, the values of the social system he or she leads, the values of others with whom the leader interacts and leads, and the values of the larger context within which that system exists. While this may seem like an overwhelming prospect, the concept of "Presencing" as articulated by Otto Scharmer, Senior Lecturer at the Massachusetts Institute of Technology, is helpful in getting to the core of Systems leadership. Presencing is "the capacity to know based on a sense of interconnected wholes and from the deepest source of self."[66] The Systems leader's awareness and appreciation is of a very wide scope, owing to a holistic worldview. The Systems Leadership style can accommodate a widening of scale to include even a global scope. Systems Leadership is not confined to multinational or global organizations by any means, but those environments require a perception that supports the assumptions of working with a system at that level of extension and complexity. Values of such a grand scope should be recognized as always being in a state of aspiration, that is, we may be able to operate with these values with some degree of competence, but true fulfillment will always escape our grasp. Many of the values that contribute directly to Systems leadership require interactive participation with others in a sustained way, which do not share this style, and are indeed looking for something entirely different in a leader, for example, a "hero," with an Individual-Center style. It is the responsibility of the Systems leader to reach across all views to understand what the world looks like from other perspectives, and in addition, to influence those who do not hold priorities critical to the objectives of the group to include those values, regardless of a person's individual perspective. This must be done with care so as to allow each person to maintain his or her own native perceptual view and individual values. We will have more to say on this in the section on group and organizational alignment.

The Values Field

The combined or aggregate of the perspectives constitutes what we call a "Values Field."

Each perspective conceivably holds hundreds of values, so what you see here is a selection of values that are representative of each perspective. Our work with professionals in an extremely wide variety of organizations,

66 C. Otto Scharmer, *Theory U* (Cambridge, MA: Society for Organizational Learning, Inc., 2007),183-229.

across nationalities, cultures, industries, non-profit, education, and government has taught us that any model or assessment must be both free from bias, as much as possible, and be representative of values that are commonly found in life across the board.

The restrictions of a printed page have dictated the size and format of the perspectives and respective values. Trying to maintain the circular model results in technological challenges that hamper its use, so we have made a concession and present the values field in a more conventional way, with a note that the mode actually is circular. The values field, with the currently used 102 values is shown below.

GROUNDING	FAMILY	MANAGEMENT	RELATIONAL	SYSTEMS	EXPANSION
Affection	*Belief*	*Achievement*	*Acceptance*	*Beauty*	*Altruism*
Curiosity	*Belonging*	*Authority*	*Analogy*	*Collaboration*	*Detachment*
Food and Shelter	*Caretaking*	*Charity*	*Balance*	*Community*	*Global Enfranchisement*
Kindness	*Discipline*	*Competence*	*Being Present*	*Development*	*Human Rights*
Maintenance	*Duty*	*Competition*	*Choice*	*Dialogue*	*Inspiring Others*
Obedience	*Economic Security*	*Decisiveness*	*Commitment*	*Empowering Others*	*Mind-Body Integration*
Physical Functioning	*Fairness*	*Efficiency*	*Courage*	*Equality*	*Nonviolence*
Safety	*Honesty*	*Financial Success*	*Creativity*	*Exploration*	*Planetary Ecology*
Self-Restraint	*Legacy*	*Hierarchal Ability*	*Diversity*	*Flexibility*	*Reconciliation*
Sensuality	*Loyalty*	*Informing*	*Empathy*	*Innovation*	*Simplification*
Wonder	*Patience*	*Managing*	*Independence*	*Integrity*	*Spirituality*
	Playfulness	*Order*	*Intimacy*	*Interdependence*	
	Recognition	*Patriotism*	*Learning*	*Intuition*	
	Respect	*Predictability*	*Listening*	*Partnership*	
	Self-Sacrifice	*Problem Solving*	*Openness*	*Service*	
	Self-Worth	*Productivity*	*Personal Growth*	*Simultaneity*	
	Stability	*Quality*	*Questioning*	*Strategy*	
	Tradition	*Rationality*	*Reflection*	*Sustainability*	
		Recreation	*Risk*		
		Responsibility	*Search for Meaning*		
		Rule of Law	*Trust*		
		Self-Confidence	*Well-Being*		

Fig. 12 - The Values Perspective Field

As we noted in the section on Characteristics of Values, there are potentially thousands of human values. We use this set because they are relatively easily understood and can be defined in straightforward terms. For example, they are not overly large or hard to define concepts such as "love," nor are they combined concepts. We have found them described in many sources and found them adequate to the purposes of individual coaching and values identification and alignment within groups. Nevertheless, there are a lot more than are shown above, so if you do not see one of your own, personal values, we invite you to do a little homework. Develop as succinct and short a definition as you possibly can and then consider, given the descriptions of the perspectives found above, where you think it fits. Then, go ahead and pencil your value into the perspective on the chart.

Minding the Gap

Seeing the perspectives arrayed in the Values Field (fig. 12) makes it easier to recognize an important factor in understanding how values operate in human interactions. We mentioned early on that there is an advantage in conserving the linear stage model adopted and modified by the values theorists discussed above. Using this representation, it is especially easy to see that each perspective contains values that are clustered within a domain of meaning. As we have shown, each perspective comprises a worldview with specific characteristics.

Grounding	Family	Management	Relational	Systems	Expansion
Surviving, and fulfilling the most basic needs. This is our most fundamental view toward the world, and is necessary for a solid life foundation.	Values in this perspective reflect kinship and social affiliation, and our most basic relationship to self and others.	These values are necessary for establishing and maintaining stability, and influencing within hierarchal contexts.	These values emphasize individual responsibility for developing one's own potential, as well as the quality of one's relationships with others.	These values address our interaction within dynamic groups, networks and larger systems, and influencing beyond our individual scope.	Values in this perspective act as guides to the future, our goals and aspirations. These values "pull" us toward globally-oriented vision.

Fig. 13 — The Values Perspectives

We have seen that each of us tends to see the world from one of these perspectives. This does not prevent us from establishing "reach," which we define as being able to hold values across the values field, regardless of our core perspective. In practice, we frequently discern perspective "gaps." This can mean two things. First, the perspective we hold will tend to color our perceptions and how we define the individual values we hold, regardless of where they belong in the values field. This means that we will see the world differently from people who hold a core perspective which is different from our own. These differences can show up in our relationships, at work, and in society. It may mean that even though we share the same value, for example Honesty, we may define it differently from the standpoint of our core perspective than someone with a different core perspective. And, we may fail to recognize what we define as 'honesty' in the actions of that other person and, vice-versa. Because of the nature of how the perspectives are clustered (which we will discuss further in Part IV), whereas "adjacent" perspectives may represent a significant difference in worldview, worldviews that are separated by one or more perspectives will tend to represent an even greater degree of felt difference between the people holding them. We have all experienced significant misunderstanding and conflict in our lives. Very often, such failures are attributable to a difference in values perspective.

Second, if our own values reach does not include some values energy in perspectives other than our core, we may lack the drive to develop skills that will enable us to realize our own values. We may also simply fail to value individuals, groups, and institutions whose core perspective may be one in which we have a values gap.

All of these perspectives represent energies that each of us needs to be effective in our lives, regardless of what our core perspective may be. When working with values, it can be vital to identify such gaps. When working with values with individuals or in group settings, this is a basic observation that a coach or consultant can call into attention, to aid understanding of how the individual or group may best address communication challenges and objectives, and to make conscious values choices. The implications of the gap are something to keep in mind as we move on to delve more deeply into values dynamics in the next part of this book.

Part IV: Interpreting and Working with Values

What can you do with values? More to the point, what exactly is the Values Perspective, what does it do (as well as what it does not do); and how can it be used?

The Values Perspective is a theoretical structure for understanding how values operate. It is supported by a survey (described below). The survey is useful, for the person who takes it and receives an individualized report with guidelines for understanding and working with their own highest-priority values; for coaches, who receive a deeper level of data to apply in the one-on-one coaching process; and for the internal or external consultant, who receives an aggregated group report that can be used to guide values alignment with small groups or indeed an entire organization (we assure that coaches and consultants understand the theory as a requirement for using these reports). However, using the survey and these reports is not necessary. We use the theory constantly without surveying, and we find its explanatory and projective power to be useful in facilitating generative discussions, and its key dynamics relatively easy to explain. Part IV will concentrate on the key dynamics of the theory and model. First, we will describe the objectives of the Values Perspective survey.

The Values Perspective Survey

The purpose of the Values Perspective Survey is twofold: identifying one's core perspective and one's top priority values. The survey is always directed toward an individual, who, through conscious choices, is answering the question, "What is most important?" When we aggregate group responses, the snapshot that is provided operates like a histogram, showing the distribution of energy available to a group in each perspective, as well as gaps or areas that in discussion, may be agreed upon as areas in need of a greater deliberate expenditure of energy, which is accomplished by simply reprioritizing values. Easy to say, but in fact, values *can* be consciously chosen, and when such a determination is made by an individual, or by agreement in a group (or, by fiat where such a mandate is well-supported and will be accepted by a majority of the population in question), the newly-selected value can become a watchword for decision-making, developmental priorities, and compensation, to name a few.

The survey provides a relatively simple mechanism that helps the person taking it to reflect on value choices. Importantly, this is not a forced-choice mechanism; in other words, values are not presented in such a way as to directly compete with each other. Nor is it in any way a psychometric instrument with psychological rules underlying how values are presented, weighted, or judged relative to a "best" values set. Sometimes, the choice between two values is challenging. Frequent reactions from people who take the survey are, "It took me hours, and I never thought so much about what is important to me before;" "Just the process of taking it really made me reflect." For some people, it is less challenging: "I breezed right through it, and yes, these are my values." (And occasionally, "These are my values! How did you know?")

It is vital to respect the choices of each person as being as valid as any and every other person's choices. The survey results (each individual taking the Values Perspective survey immediately receives a detailed, personal report) can be powerfully important, because they tap into deeply seated energy. After those choices have been made, we can then begin to work with them, with the caveat that we may not infer conclusions that are inappropriate. For example, the Values Perspective survey is *not* a personality assessment, so we may not infer personality characteristics like extraversion and introversion. It is *not* a skills assessment, so we may not infer behavioral competencies, even though we may infer general preferred-style patterns, based on various groups of values selected. We might infer a general leadership style, as discussed above, but we cannot know how well or how poorly one executes a particular style, nor indeed whether this style might be warranted by context; nor can we tell if one has developed competencies in other styles that are not specified as important priorities for a particular person. The Values Perspective is *not* an emotional assessment, so we cannot infer emotional maturity or lack of it based on the selection of particular values, such as self-restraint or empathy. It is *not* a moral assessment, so we cannot infer that someone is dishonest if they have not selected honesty as a top priority value, nor can we infer that someone is spiritual because he or she has selected spirituality as a top value (the case may be that a person wants to become spiritual, whatever that means for that person). The survey is a tool that can be used by an individual to reflect on his or her values and their import in personal and professional life and by a trained coach or consultant, to engender dialogue leading to understanding and appropriate action. When we aggregate the data from individual surveys, for people belonging to the same group, we can say, "These are the values that are important to the group in general," and, based on that description, we may develop tentative or working hypotheses about the operational group culture, which can then be confirmed or disconfirmed by the group. But we cannot infer, and the theory does not prescribe, what the group's values should be. That is up to the group.

Values are powerful, ambiguous, and personal, and diving into a group discussion that engages these three factors can be a recipe for disaster if the facilitator or discussion-leader is unprepared for the inevitable release of energy, whether the facilitator/leader is aware of it in the moment or not, so we believe it is necessary to be both complete and careful in our treatment of values. We do this work because working with values can be extremely rewarding. Working with values is working with and honoring what people hold dear and often suggesting ways for them to engage more fully and more effectively with their values and their lives.

Our first objective in this part of the book is to provide you with an understanding of the various, principal ways in which values can be organized. We will revisit some of the concepts we have previously discussed, in particular values perspectives, but our discussion will be more detailed and will explore common questions and issues that arise in regard to how values are organized. Then, we will discuss the relationship between values and behavior, because ultimately, it is through behavior, which for us includes language use, that we identify and fulfill our values choices.

No "Best" Perspective

People sometimes ask (and if not, we learn they are often wondering), "Am I in the right place on the chart?" "Is this the best perspective?"

Historically, moral (i.e., values) development has been assumed to track with age/life stage development; that is to say, it is assumed to be a function of the basic physical and psychological maturation pattern that is the norm for our species. So the logical extension of this assumption leads to the conclusion that in a healthy life one would start with a Grounding perspective and end with an Expansion perspective. We believe this is both inaccurate and inappropriate. Our own experience with our clients indicates that age, development, and values development are closely connected in early life, but once adolescence is reached, they do not follow a similar process with regard to values formation, and so cannot be directly compared. We do believe (or hope) that people generally grow wiser as they get older, gaining experience and competence. But we recognize that as adults, many people become habituated and routinized to a great degree, and as we sometimes ask those in the creativity and leadership development programs we lead, "Have you had 20 years of experience, or one year of experience, 20 times?"

Our point is that as adults, some people do not engage in learning and development, some do because life events force them into it, and some engage in that sort of change voluntarily. That is why we believe that values identification should not be used as an assessment of an individual's developmental attainments, but it can be a useful and effective tool for subsequent development choices.

However, this is not quite the same as shifting from one core perspective to another. We reject the assumption that people must move from one perspective to another as if the perspectives were sequentially better, or morally "higher" (increasingly more moral) in order to fulfill the artificial requirements of the traditional linear model. The Values Perspective model, and our observation and experience indicate that neither change in worldviews (i.e., perspectives) nor development work that way.

There isn't any generally optimum or "best" perspective. Most people fall into the 'middle' four perspectives of Family, Management, Relational or Systems. Within that set, more people have a core perspective in Family, or Management; there tends to be a lower number of people with a Relational or Systems core perspective. Any of these can be seen to be functional and appropriate. A core identification that is in Grounding or Expansion, either looking at the model on the left or far to the right in its linear presentation, may create problems for people when they need to access their values at the other end of the model. Being more than one stage removed from other people who have a focus in a different perspective will create some tension due to the fact that their relative perceptions will be quite different. For example, it has been our experience when working with people in leadership positions who hold a comparatively "visionary" set of values, primarily from the Systems or Expansion perspectives, that some of them have an extremely difficult time in two areas. The first is a difficulty in attending to the mundane and regulatory or managerial parts of life that keep things running with some stability and enough routine to create confidence on the part of people around them that their lives and work are on sufficiently stable ground. The second is a difficulty in communicating with others who do not hold similar core perspectives. They may literally fail to "value" the views of people whose focus lies in the Family, Management, or Relational perspectives. In this sort of situation, miscommunication or lack of appreciation is not a necessary outcome, but it is what we often observe if the person lacks the awareness that they must temporarily adopt a different perspective so they can relate effectively to others. This is an indication of gaps between perspective views. If there is any one perspective that seems to need the most attention, it is the Relational perspective. That is the perspective that is home to the values that move people toward skills that will allow them to develop and maintain relationships with others who have different worldviews.

Instead of "Which perspective is best?" the more useful questions in helping people interpret the practical implications of their focus location regardless of where it appears are, "How great is your reach? Can you access all of your potentially important values, and can you relate to others that do not share your perspective on the world?" Knowing what our core perspective is gives us a tool for both our own development and for effective relationships.

Reach

Reach refers to being able to activate values across the values field (shown in Fig. 12, above), which accomplishes the support necessary for a given value, and provides opportunity to exercise our understanding though a value, and perhaps even a perspective that is different than our original values and perspective. We will talk more below about what we mean by supporting a given value, through the mechanisms of linking and clusters. Most people, and most groups, have values they regard as high-priority outside of their core perspective. This is healthy and necessary, since values do not operate in isolation; rather, they cluster in various ways to give us access to the energies we need to be competent in all life situations. Very often, people who have taken the Values Perspective survey and opted to discuss their results with a coach or counselor will find that they want to give more attention to values that they may not have previously considered important. As we have said, values can be *chosen*. At the same time, reach does not imply that we can or should work with more and more values. We would quickly arrive at the point of diminishing returns, and find that we are likely spread too thin, and are not being effective implementing much of anything.

Reach requires intention and consideration. Why would you want to prioritize a particular value that is associated with a perspective not close to your own? The answer is often, "To facilitate communication with others," or, "To expand my own awareness and capabilities." Whatever your reason, before any decisions are made, and actions taken, we advise vetting your choices with others, or at least one other person, to check your assumptions and expectations. Such a discussion should be structured such that you are able to clarify your intentions, and keep the question in mind, "What is most important and why?"

Overall, remember that in regard to our natural or native values identity, we may tend to orbit for periods of time, like planets around the gravitational pull of a perspective, cluster, or even a single high priority value. We do not stay in one location in the values universe. Our attention shifts quickly and it may shift often, depending on the situational needs presented to us. As we move our attention, we may find ourselves gravitating toward a value to which we give a high priority, but which we do not actually understand very well or do not have the skills to support. When that occurs, we are engaged in our own values development.

Adding or Re-prioritizing Values

When we say values can be chosen, this means reprioritization of some of the energy we currently expend. We can think of the Values Field as an energy map for a given person, and while in different contexts in life we can "work overtime," we only have 100% of our energy. We cannot create more than that. However, we can re-distribute that energy. We may decide that a particular value that is important to us may need the support of other values. For example, valuing financial success for some may require also valuing economic security as a more foundational condition if the life structures are not already in place for taking steps toward more financial reward. If what we presently have is inadequate, or we know little about what it takes to build a sound financial foundation, we can decide to add a value to that foundation and consciously create the intention to expend energy seeking and developing the skills to support it. By adding an appropriate supporting value, we have improved our chances of attaining a desired potential.

At the same time, since we now are putting energy and time into the accomplishment of a new, supporting value, we are not able to put the same energy into all of our other existing priority values at the same level. So we must decide what to de-emphasize. That too, is a part of values development.

This process may seem simple, but in practice it always requires a trial and error process that allows us to both develop and test our skills, but also to test the interconnection between new and the existing values. Most of the time there are unexpected consequences from making such adjustments, so this process requires revisiting, reflecting on, perhaps asking others for feedback, and refining both our choices and our behaviors.

Values Development

Ironically, by creating a model and survey that does not attempt to measure development, we are now, nevertheless, able to freely engage in development using the awareness and understanding of what our own priorities are. It is our contention that by taking the simple first step of identifying priorities in a non-judgmental assessment, a person is then able to be fair minded about engaging in his or her own development and his or her participation in a given group, and its development.

It is our experience that if development is assessed first, i.e., what "level" might a person have reached in a hierarchally-presented schema, then a fair assessment of priorities is nearly impossible because a person has been, in essence, set up, biased in an a priori way toward (or against) certain values and perspectives. Many people, approaching such an assessment, will make an effort to give the "right" or what they believe to be, the expected answers. This is one of the primary reasons we have created the Values Perspective, because we simply could not find an assessment that did not, in effect, value one developmental stage or worldview over another, which always implies a judgment of attainment or relative worthiness. We witnessed, many times, group members receive results of any number of assessment instruments, and immediately do two things: consider the implications of the results in terms of a grade (as in a school paper or test), and then turn to a neighbor participant and compare results. The tacit, or sometimes explicit discussion that resulted was often about who's results are "better." We found that to be counter-productive to development, both individual and at the group level.

Development in general refers to change; usually in regard to growth in areas in which we are not proficient, but certainly not confined to that. In real life development is a cyclical process, in which we may visit and revisit values in different ways throughout one's life or throughout the life-span of a group or organization. It can also be a messy process, full of moments in which we might ask ourselves, "Haven't I been here before?" In the course of a healthy life, the answer is likely "Yes." Because of their dynamic nature, working with values is complex. There is a continual tension between oversimplifying on one hand and getting too detailed and mechanical about how they work on the other. Our work has shown us that values can be organized so as to provide us with better understanding, and eventually tools for living in ways that more fully take advantage of our natural potential, and ways in which we can change the way we live, if we so choose. In the following sections, we will describe basic values mechanisms, and provide some tools that can help to make the process of development more coherent, deliberate and effective. These mechanisms tend to be in operation whether we are conscious of them or not. Awareness of them will help you to make conscious decisions about your life plan, and as well as helping you to understand what choices you may need to make when life does not go as planned.

Value Clusters and Development

One of their fundamental characteristics is that values do not exist in isolation, but tend to link or cluster together. In the previous section, we have described one such clustering, the values perspectives, how they frame our understanding and perceptions, and how they function. And indeed, we will continue this discussion below because perspectives are the basic organizing concept for values. However, we will also show other ways to organize values that are useful and informative, for example, value-to-value combinations or linkages, where one specific value supports another, which in turn may support a third, and forth, and so on. These linkages may be simple, one-way relationships like a track (think of a pathway across the values field), or they may be reciprocal and complex. Identifying these kinds of linkages may lead to placing greater energy toward values that may previously have constituted a 'gap,' where a value or values may have needed attention to better serve an individual's or group's goals and intentions. The Values Perspectives survey is very helpful in such cases, as it can show not only where values energy is consciously focused, but where it is missing, i.e., not receiving the attention that perhaps it should, given what an individual or group may want to accomplish. Change or shift can occur from one core perspective to another. We will also discuss how perspectives can be grouped together into larger clusters we call the Foundation, Focus, and Vision values sets. This is a particularly useful rubric, which, once grasped, can be one of the simplest and most powerful values concepts to convey to others. Too, grouping value perspectives into Foundation, Focus and Vision clusters can be a powerful tool for managing development, for individuals and for small and large groups.

Linkages and Tracks

Values tend to link, one value to the next, in support of still other values, or they may link reciprocally, supporting each other. Indeed, there are several ways, not all of them linear and not all of them involving "contiguous" or neighboring perspectives, in which we tend to create potentially dynamic links and groupings of values that may lead us to choices that involve development and may ultimately lead to a change in perspective:

- One value may simply lead directly, by logical extension, to another by being an expansion or further development of the same theme or topic. For example, most people associate the values of honesty (Family perspective) and integrity (Systems perspective).
- One value may act as a prerequisite to another, and may actually lead to several other values by reason of logical extension or association. For example, the value of respect (Family perspective), especially in a group context, can be seen as a precondition for trust (Relational perspective).
- The skills and behaviors associated with one value may be generalized to another value, which creates, at least in the mind of the person holding those values, a natural link between the two. For example, commitment (Relational perspective) may, for many, form a reciprocal link with interdependence (Systems perspective).
- A given situation may require a combination of values to address a specific need which may, in turn trigger awareness of a value in a different location in the values field. For example, the values of recognition and economic security (Family perspective) could together trigger the valuing of achievement (Management perspective).

- We may emphasize the combinations of certain values because of personality or other cognitive styles or preferences. Native styles, preferences, and talents tend to lead us to focus our attention or response in distinct ways. How we are disposed to place our attention or to respond to stimuli tends to direct us naturally toward priorities that show up as values that cluster or link together. For example, a Thinking preference as defined by the Myers-Briggs personality type preference theory may show up in the selection of values such as fairness (Family perspective), rationality, and problem solving (Management perspective).

- A combination of two or more values may create a relationship or a sort of dialogue in terms of our attention and energy. The result of this may lead to a third value that can be either a synthesis sort of combination, or a compromise of the two (or more) original values. For example, physical functioning (Grounding perspective) and recreation (Management perspective) may combine to support the value of well-being (Relational perspective).

- A number of values may be identified that form a pathway across the values field. This is often the case when activating one value may be seen to require supporting values to be called into activation. Activation of such a "values track" may also create the conditions for accessing a more aspirational value. (See the example below of a "trust track.")

We have talked about the importance of reach across the values perspectives. One mechanism that can be very useful in individual coaching and group consulting is the identification of a set of linked values that indeed reach across the perspectives. This can be very important to an individual or group attaining a goal, for example, the creation of trust within a team that may not be sufficiently supported by values that are highest-priority within the group. The concept of a values track comes from the work of Brian Hall, who understands it to be a natural mechanism for growth.[67]

Example: The Trust Track

Trust is a value that is commonly cited in professional situations as being critical for success, regardless of context. An individual or group

67 Brian P. Hall, *Values Shift*. Rockport, MA, Twin Lights Publications, 1995, 76-82.

may select trust as a high-priority value, but that value alone is not going to enable them to achieve what they value. When asked about the value based behaviors of group members who are trusted, others perceived such people to be good listeners, and, often, as a part of listening, they reciprocate. Openness can be very important when others are sharing information which may render them vulnerable, and reciprocation with openness may be felt, in a sense, to equalize the risk. Openness tends to include the appropriate sharing of personal information, or personal opinion, thus, serves to build solid relationships. Listening and being open with relevant information are both supporting values to the value of trust. All three are found within the Relational perspective. Still, Reach requires that values from additional perspectives be in operation, so that we are able to communicate and influence across perspectives. Informing, a value in the Management perspective, is a necessary supporting value. Its definition is simple: providing information, yet its impact may be best seen when relevant information may be perceived by others as being withheld, which can create disequilibrium and distrust, as people begin to speculate, in the absence of information, what might be going on. Now, when we look into the Family perspective, the value of respect can be seen as foundational to building and fostering trust. The Foundational values cluster will be discussed more below. Naturally, how we intend to treat people simply as human beings will impact our ability to create trust.

Interestingly, once we understand what supports the value of trust, we may begin to look to what a solid foundation of trust may allow us to create that might be at present aspirational; in other words, something we want and do not know how to bring into reality, or something we may not yet be aware of as a desired possibility. Listening, openness, and trust are Relational perspective values. If we now look to the Systems perspective, we find the value of collaboration can also be seen to be supported by the track of values we have just identified. Collaboration may be one of the more significant aspirational values for today's organizations, which require innovation. Yet, if trust is not in place, collaboration will be short-lived or impossible.

If we isolated the values just discussed, the 'track' would look something like this:

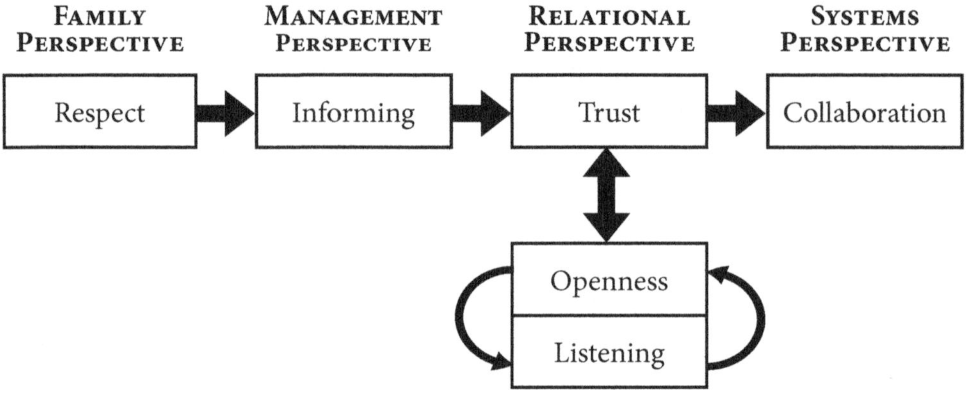

Fig. 14 — Trust Track

Since trust is often an issue for groups we work with, we use this track often. It demonstrates very quickly how each value is necessary for the entire organizational structure to work effectively, and when each value is behaviorally produced within a team or work group, the end result is almost automatically collaboration.

And of course other values might be included, and some of those we have identified here might be excluded because any values track must be created for a specific group or person, where each value is identified and vetted by those using it. Otherwise, at best, this is just an interesting exercise. Our point is to show you how tracks can form.

In practice, the formation of a values track tends to begin with a question or hypothesis. A values coaching or alignment process requires an examination of an individual's or a group's highest priority values vis-à-vis their goals and aspirations. In the above example, trust frequently appears among high-priority values selected by groups. This presents an opportunity to initiate dialogue about how trust can be created and sustained, given the unique make-up, context and mandate of the group. The question must be asked, what supports a value that is said to be important. How will that value be activated? What other values in the values field or, indeed any values identified by an individual or group, may need to become high priorities in order to transform valuing into realistic choices and resultant behavioral commitments? The personalized report that results when anyone takes the Values Perspective survey asks a set of specific questions about each of the high-priority values selected, to provide the querent many ways to think about how selected values may be effectively activated.

The supporting value links in a track can move either direction because there is no best, or preferred perspective. There may be multiple values within a perspective in operation, so the track can even begin to look much more like a web, like the trust example, above, which is perfectly acceptable. However, we have found that if we can keep this sort of values organization as simple as possible, it is much more likely to be useful for those whose values are in operation. Perhaps, four to seven values can be organized into a track that makes sense and can serve as a guideline for development. Within groups, this further requires that agreement is reached, about 1) how the values in the track are defined and understood by that group, 2) what each of those values would look like in behavioral terms for that group, and 3) what steps would need to be taken to achieve the desired results, for example, the attainment of greater trust between group members. We will discuss the process for group values alignment further in Part V.

In our own work, we tend to develop these linkages based on themes and use a value in the linkage that seems particularly important for the group to use as a title, like "trust track." But, there are no hard and fast rules for their identification and creation. What is important is to create the conditions for dialogue—whether an internal dialogue prompted by a Values Perspective survey report, a dialogue between an individual and a coach, a group dialogue, or indeed an organization-wide project—that will result in mutual understanding and agreements that will lead to action that is aligned to specific goals.

When we aggregate the values for an entire group or organization, and then proceed to develop these structures using the values that show up in the aggregate reports, the discussions can be quite rich because the group can identify representative behaviors for each value, and thereby, both validate its operation, and talk about what behaviors they feel support group effectiveness with regard to a value as well as those that do not.

The Dynamics of Values Perspectives

The first step is to figure out what is going on for you, and the first step of the process is the identification of one's primary perceptual framework, or perspective.

One, or for some, two, of the six general perspectives operate as a worldview for the individual, and when generally shared by a group, operates as a worldview for that group, constituting the main characteristics of the group or organizational culture. But, it is vital not to fall prey to placing people in a sort of rigid box and run the risk of stereotyping. We recognize that sometimes value priorities don't fit neatly into one single perspective or another. Indeed, in the Values Perspective survey, identifying one's core perspective is a matter of determining which perspective receives the largest proportion of an individual's energy and attention. At times, that energy can be nearly equally divided between two perspectives. A report we call the Values Field Report, which coaches and consultants can access, provides that information. In those cases where the values energy is concentrated in more than one perspective, a conversation with the individual (or group) will usually surface which perspective the person identifies with the most as his or her native perspective. Too, in such cases, the person's energy may be seen to cycle between the two perspectives depending on the situation. More frequently than not, a dual perspective will be seen to concentrate between two non-contiguous perspectives, for example Family and Relational, or even Family and Systems. When examined with the person, this may be seen as their ability to reach across the perspectives to access energies appropriate to their intentions and needs. A person with a dual Family/Systems perspective orientation may be better equipped to communicate with, and if need be, influence, people with either of these perspectives than others who may be more energetically focused in one or the other, literally because they are able to *value* their perspective. This may be an advantage, for example, when a person who is accustomed to operating from a Systems perspective in their immediate work setting, may be called upon to summon a different perspective with another work function, or in family life at home and in community and may feel relatively at ease when stepping from one into the other. They may also be able to act as a sort of translator or go-between to stakeholders with differing perspectives. And/or, this may be indicative of some tension in certain circumstances, when people may consciously be striving toward operationalizing values in one perspective or another, for example, if they have been promoted to a position of greater scope, or perhaps, are being called upon to expend more energy toward children or aging parents. A dual perspective orientation that is non-contiguous may also point up to the person a need to place energy in the intervening perspective(s). This entails a dynamic we will discuss further, below.

Remember, the primary objective of the values Perspective model is to help people understand how their values energy is concentrated or distributed, and not to ensure that people are assigned to a category that may confine them to a sort of box, and where values are concerned, we often see the natural variety of humans come to light. We often tell the people we are working with, the question is not "where you are," in regard to your perspective, but "how big is your reach?" That is, can you effectively communicate with people whose core perspective is different than your own?

Changing From One Core Perspective To Another

As adults, our worldview, represented by our core perspective, tends to be stable, in contrast to our priority values—the order of which is very dynamic, depending on the situation we find ourselves in. But, perspectives do change. People change, and they do so for a wide variety of specific reasons, but in a general sense they change for two basic reasons: development or stress. But as we will see, the difference between the two can be difficult to actually describe.

When enough values in a different perspective are selected as priority values by an individual, his or her core perspective changes. The first one or two changes in core perspective should occur as a normal pattern of human growth from infancy to adult capability, as identified in the classic psychological stage models reviewed above. These changes can be gradual, or more sudden, for example, when a young person first discovers idealism and his or her focus may jolt into the Vision cluster without much support from values development in the usual Focus area. Normal adult responsibilities tend to pull the individual back toward the typical core perspective. Once we have begun our professional lives, change in core perspective perception often happens as a result of finding ourselves in a challenging situation, but are unable to manage successfully without undergoing a change in focus. A shift in perspective can be associated with some anxiety since it follows that we will not likely have developed the same degree of skill to support the values associated in a new focus stage as in a previous, more comfortable one. Development is messy, and the awareness of this frees us from trying to locate or fix a position with too much certainty. Identifying a core perspective is useful, but some tolerance for our own situational needs for flexibility is also important.

Development does involve change in values in two ways. We may experience a relatively sudden shift in core perspectives. Or, more incrementally, as relationships or linkages form between specific values in adjacent perspectives.

When a change of one's core perspective occurs, it represents a fundamental shift in perception. It can be heralded by dramatic events—

like assuming one's first professional position, going through a personal crisis, experiencing a profound spiritual insight (like recognizing in a flash of awareness one's calling in life or one's culpability in a negative life outcome), being thrust into a position requiring one to exercise great authority, or being precipitated into a mid-life crisis, all events that have a sort of "no going back" imperative to them—the shift is rarely accomplished in a moment. Moreover, while we may prioritize values that are recognizable as thematically related across perspectives, prioritizing a few values within a different perspective, either to the right or left of what has been the core perspective may naturally draw more attention and energy in that direction, to the extent that the core changes.

This sort of change is very similar to Thomas Kuhn's description of how major scientific paradigm or perspectives change.[68] From the standpoint of the existing paradigm —in this case core perspective—the world seems normal, and the individual seeks to maintain this perspective because of a fundamental assumption that this is the correct way to understand and from which to act. Incoming stimuli that require skills and understanding that have not previously existed for the person may cause him or her to responded by moving toward values within the existing core perspective that have not been developed. However, at some point a realization occurs that the existing core perspective will no longer suffice to deal with current reality. As was mentioned above, this is usually marked with some sort of milestone event, but in fact the process itself is not confined to an event, and may take some time to occur. Meanwhile, the individual is continually being pulled to operate with values outside his or her own core perspective, some of which may already have been to some extent activated by the ongoing process of values linking across perspectives in response to life circumstances. When one adopts a different core perspective, a feeling of crisis is often experienced because each perspective carries with it an inherent "lens" constituting a world view, and from that new perspective, one will find that all previously held values have likely changed their meaning somewhat. This can be a very disconcerting and unnerving experience. For example, a perspective shift from Management to Relational can mean just that: what we have managed before, with the expectation that stability is to be greatly valued, may shift to a need, especially at first, to cope with seeing things—and

---

68 Thomas Kuhn, *The Structure of Scientific Revolutions* (Chicago: University of Chicago Press, 1962).

especially relationships—as being more relative, dynamic and context-sensitive, which may in turn require increased tolerance of risk. Kuhn suggests this shift is always accompanied by a crisis. We would suggest this is often true, at least in terms of the internal shift that occurs for the person involved, but there are certainly milestone events that are positive, even if they feel like a sort of crisis. Ask any new parent, for example, if they feel prepared for the future and if they feel like the world has shifted under their feet at some point.

With regard to a more gradual process of perspective change, simply desiring a different perspective is not sufficient to create the fundamental shift in perception that changing one's core perspective represents. However, if we begin to prioritize an increasing number of values in an adjacent perspective, at some point a sort of critical mass will be reached, and we will experience a fundamental shift in perspective as our home or core perspective changes. The caution that must always accompany this shift is to be sure of two things. First, we are not leaving a perspective view without genuine behavioral competency for at least some values associated with that perspective. Second, we do not forget what the world looked like from that perspective. If we fail at this second challenge, we will lose the ability to communicate effectively with people who do hold this original perspective, which by the way, Kuhn suggests is usually the case, and is what we have often observed with changes in values perspectives.

A gradual developmental shift, based on the process described above, might not be experienced as disorienting. However, the reality is that it can very often feel more precipitous. We often work with people who, for example, have been promoted into a position, usually senior leadership, for which they have little experience, and are approaching it with both elation and serious trepidation ("But I'm not ready, I don't know what to do"). In this sort of case the process is similar, in that they must start prioritizing values from the new perspective with whose operation they may be unfamiliar, but in practical terms, they have little choice in the matter and will naturally feel overwhelmed for some period of time, which may in fact stretch into years. In addition, they may need to work with several unfamiliar values and skill sets simultaneously.

The natural process is for each person to look for links between these new values and their more familiar values for support.

Value Dynamics: Foundation, Focus and Vision Clusters

We have addressed how values can be structured in perspective groupings or clusters and what it means for an individual or group to focus in a core values perspective. We are not confined to a single perspective, no matter what this core perspective may be, but always hold values in many perspectives. Values cluster and link together in a variety of ways in addition to that of being organized by perspectives. With that in mind, we will describe three basic value clusters. These clusters are adapted from the work of Hall and Tonna, who have articulated how each person's or group's value systems can be organized into three distinct and interacting groups.[69] We have found Hall's terms for these clusters, Foundation, Focus, and Vision, to be useful, and most people can readily understand them with minimal explanation. These clusters are operational for both individuals and groups of any size.

Foundation Cluster

This group contains values and associated skills that are usually developed early in life as a part of normal psychological and physical development, and often can operate in the background. However, most people are aware of the importance of their foundation, just not the specifics of what goes into it. The skills that support foundation values may be acquired at any time in one's life, so if as a result of a stressful event you find you cannot put some of your foundation values into practice as well as you expected, there is no time like the present to start learning. An interesting feature of values in this cluster is that they may operate without conscious awareness until some situational need triggers them.

When we use a survey in doing values work, we are by definition measuring *conscious* value choices. We often find that relatively few values are selected from this area. This may occur because those values are being sufficiently addressed—probably in routine ways—and are operating unconsciously. Yet, we may be taken by surprise when, at times when foundational skills are required, we are not in connection with and do not actively value the concepts that would lead us to maintain basic psychological attitudes or physical skills that we may need, or to otherwise fulfill foundational needs. For this reason, it is important to review the Foundation Cluster once in a while to be sure that values are in

69 Hall, 84.

place to allow us to appropriately address needs arising in times of crisis or stress, or during life transitions.

Longstanding research has shown that 70% of organizational learning comes from challenging work assignments.[70] Learning comes, in many cases, when a situation arises that demands attention to Foundation. Recently conducted cross-cultural research named a number of sources of learning that made leaders better. The most oft-cited source of learning, by managers from China, India, Singapore and the U.S., is a boss or supervisor. Sometimes superior/subordinate relationships are very challenging indeed, and dealing with a boss who pushes your buttons can result in a debilitating loss of self-worth until you are able to change the situation, or respond to it. As anyone knows, such challenges are very frequent in the world of work, as are feelings of failure when a subordinate is insubordinate in a personally challenging manner, particularly when simply firing the person, for legal and other reasons, is not the option of first resort. Turnaround is named as one of the strongest learning situations in India, China, and the U.S. Being assigned to effect turnaround may require discovery of how very deep a systemic problem may lie, and addressing faults in the very foundation of a function or an entire company. In China, mistakes are cited as the key sources of learning.[71] Failure which may include such consequences as shipping faulty products or even worker or consumer injury and serious issues of liability often by necessity results in re-grounding in the security-oriented value perspectives, with an outcome of better policies and processes and a return or attainment to the stability values of the Management perspective as an ultimate outcome. Those companies and managers who fail to take serious account when Foundational issues arise often suffer the consequences of business collapse and/or legal culpability.

We think of Foundation cluster values metaphorically, as the foundation of the psychic 'house' we build in our lives. In spite of the fact that no one wishes to experience, or to see people they care for, experience negative life events that call for revisiting foundation values, many people when asked will say that a negative life experience brought them something of

70 Jean Brittain Leslie and Phillip Braddy, *Benchmarks* (Greensboro, NC: Center for Creative Leadership, 2013), 9, accessed October 10, 2013, http://www.ccl.org/leadership/pdf/assessments/BenchmarksTechnicalManual.pdf.

71 Meena Surie Wilson et al., "Grooming Top Leaders: Cultural Perspectives from China, India, Singapore and the United States," White Paper (Center for Creative Leadership, September, 2011), 4, accessed November 2, 2013, http://www.ccl.org/leadership/pdf/research/GroomingTopLeaders.pdf.

value. Sometimes, this gift is one of great cost, financially, psychologically, or physically (and not uncommonly, all three). However, life events that may call us into our Foundation may also present an opportunity to metaphorically rebuild it, and give more stability to the house, even allowing the personality to be, in a sense, rebuilt in such a way as to better withstand unsettling future events with perhaps less disequilibrium. For most people, this is part of a healthy life-cycle, and challenging events may be experienced as what we eventually look back upon as important and formative life junctures. These visits to the Foundation are part of what leads to learning and to maturing, and an enhanced sense of self.

Focus Cluster

Using the metaphor of the house, focus values are "where we live," whether we are aware of it or not. These are the values that guide our decisions and actions on a daily basis. The values in this area generally get most of our attention and account for most of the application of our energy. Even so, we may not be fully conscious of these values in operation in our daily lives, and a values assessment can be helpful in bringing them into conscious view. Generally, about six to nine values govern our awareness most of the time, but those are not usually confined to a given perspective. Nevertheless, we generally see how the core perspective is an expression of an individual's Focus values cluster. An individual's Focus cluster values are those he or she would be aware of and they function as highly-prioritized values on a regular basis. But our Focus is made up of many less important values as well. We simply are often not aware of them until we see them in a list or hear them in conversation, or until one of them is violated in some way, or a situation arises that requires the implementation of one of our "lesser" values, at which time it will, at least temporarily, become one of our high priority values.

The Focus area is also where we grow. Focus values operate in two basic ways. Some will be associated with skills and competencies you have already mastered, to the degree that you can legitimately call them your strengths, through which you address everyday goals and activities. These values also represent the platform of attitudes and skills from which you launch into new areas of development. The growing edge of these core values, representing potentials you have not completely mastered, leads you toward the desire to develop new skills to actualize them. These forward-looking values tend to point your attention to the ways in which you can create and grow as a person. This lagging-leading dynamic may be seen as a model for healthy development, as values previously not in conscious operation come into awareness and assume higher priority, and values that previously may have been more important recede in importance, either because the skills are attitudes associated with their effective operation become habitual and require less conscious energy, or they may simply become irrelevant to one's present life conditions.

In China, many managers remember the shift from state to private ownership and the rise of market economy required them to change focus.[72] In many cases, regulation and ordered financial processes, which require a Management perspective focus, replaced systems of political patronage that called upon being able to navigate complex relationships that were more Family perspective in nature, such as belonging and loyalty. Culturally, in China, maintaining relationships is seen as highly important and requires continued energy, so in this case, the shift in perspective is in many ways a shift of energy to accommodate Management values without entirely leaving behind the important Family perspective relationship skills that allow managers to observe and exploit subtle behavioral clues and to cement business relationships.

A note with regard to how growth and perspective change can occur in the Focus area: It cannot be over-emphasized that a movement toward the Foundation is a healthy, natural and at times absolutely necessary shift. We should have Foundational values in place at all times as a function of our reach across the values field. But, far from being negatively evaluated as regressive, relying on and moving toward values belonging to a more Foundational perspective than we may have been living with, is a part of the cyclical nature of human growth and development in the real world and as such must be valued. This is well understood, but it also cannot be over emphasized, given that many languages impose a left-to-right bias that functions well below the level of conscious understanding. Because of it, and many other deeply-embedded cultural factors, we strive toward what we think of as being higher. This, too, is healthy. Nevertheless, it must be remembered that it is not the only direction we can grow.

Vision Cluster

These are generally the values of the person we want to become, the aims we aspire to achieve, and the world we ideally want to create for ourselves and others. They exert an energetic pull toward the future. This is a good thing, because unless we are motivated by values that connect

72 Ibid., 12.

us with goals for the future, it is likely that we will simply continue in the routines that currently operate in life. Indeed, a characteristic of adult operation in the Foundation area, usually due to crisis, is that future concerns drop from consciousness or are put on hold because the compelling need is for stability. Some of the Vision values may represent competencies we may have already at least partly mastered, but it is more common that these values are associated with skills and competencies that are yet to be developed or that we may have limited access to. This may be especially true of values in the Systems and Expansion perspectives, which are characterized by more and more expansive thinking, which generally requires an increasingly broad integration of people in interdependent networks of influence.

Research shows that in the U.S., 80% of job scope increases require a manager to shoulder responsibilities that are both broader and different from the previous job. This requires a shift in perspective from Management to Systems values, like interdependence. A manager may realize, "I can't turn this big ship by myself." Lessons successfully learned mean that leaders must manage through others, and may be required to let go of previous certainties, such as the stability — or at least, the perception of stability — that is afforded by authority vested in hierarchal roles (characteristic of the Management perspective view), and put energy into securing and developing the people who will get the job done (characteristic of the Systems perspective view). [73]

Earlier, we mentioned the work of Otto Scharmer, in connection with the attitudes associated with a Systems Perspective leadership style, which is characterized by a tolerance for dynamism and ambiguity. In *Theory U*, Scharmer describes what he calls seven "cognitive spaces" or "rooms" that we pass through in the process of transforming envisioned aspirations into a set of practices. According to Scharmer, many individuals and most organizations neglect the deepest level of the process, where the bottom of the "U" descends into reflective spaces he terms "presencing." Presencing involves *letting go* of the habits, and certainties, of what has gone before; *connecting to Source*, the source inside all of us that is the home to a sense of our greatest possible potential; and *letting come*.[74] Letting something new arise can only be accomplished when something else, old attitudes, old perspectives, old values, pass into a state of lower priority. Release in this sense does not mean jettisoning prior experience. It simply means re-

73 Ibid., 10.

74 Scharmer, 38-42.

focusing on different value priorities. In this case, what was formerly in the Vision cluster becomes part of the Focus.

Not necessarily easy to do. Scharmer makes reference to two questions that Michael L. Ray, who developed the influential Stanford University business school course "Creativity in Business," asked nearly three decades ago, perhaps a bit ahead of his time, and yet, calling on perennial wisdom: "What is my Self? What is my Work?" For Ray, these questions come at the beginning of a process of liberating creativity that starts with trust. We usually think of trust as something that is developed between oneself and an individual or entity external to ourselves. But, Ray talks about trusting one's own ability to access something of value we already possess, inside ourselves.[75] This involves redefining the value of trust, and activating values such as personal growth and intuition. Putting these values into practice can be destabilizing, because they require an internal locus of control, and a shift toward a kind of responsibility that looks inside, to the self, and a lessening, when appropriate, of responsiveness to tacit or explicit external instructions about how one *should* think. This may be one of the many possible mechanisms whereby values perspectives that may have been in the Vision cluster become incorporated into the Focus cluster.

In our experience, for some, the answer to the two questions Ray, and, more recently, Scharmer, pose does not require a wholesale sloughing-off of our personality or cognitive preferences. To the extent these preferences may indeed be hard-wired, the best most of us can do, and a good job at that, is to make good on our native gifts. Nevertheless, we tend to carry a sense of Vision that, for many, is a gift of the sense of both possibility and power that is often a quality — and value — belonging to youth itself. We believe that the core of development is indeed to re-discover the gifts we are each born with. Conscious recall of these gifts tends to fall away from the list of highest-priority values, as we manage the compelling exigencies of life in a material cosmos. That list *will* change through the course of a psychologically healthy life.

Have you ever seen a roomful of dozens of lawyers brought to tears? We have. A colleague, in the course of delivering a keynote address to a regional, quarterly professional meeting, simply reminded them of why most of them undertook the considerable work of attaining a degree allowing them to practice law in the first place: to satisfy a vision of

75 Michael L. Ray, *Two Questions* (unpublished manuscript, 2004). Used with permission.

Justice. Our colleague could see that her remarks were getting a strong response. Sitting at the back of the hall, without the spotlight in our eyes, it was easy for us to see the effect of this simple re-call to consciousness of values that had led perhaps every person present to be sitting in that room. Eyes were glistening and tears were streaming on many faces (in a room where the majority of the audience were male). As people furtively glanced around at neighbors sitting at round banquet tables, they could tell that they were not alone in this unexpected and unsettling moment of recall. The meeting convener later told our colleague that many remarked afterward upon how greatly they were affected by the experience.

Relationship of the Foundation, Focus and Vision Value Clusters

The concept of clusters, such as perspectives and Foundation/Focus/Vision values, helps us manage the complexity and development dynamics of our value system and its sub-systems. Because of this dynamism, what constitutes a cluster can never be a prescribed set of values. We have seen that most commonly adults will find their Focus cluster in the Family, Management, Relational, or Systems perspectives. We hypothesize that the summit of a normal curve measuring the Focus perspectives of the general population would span the Family and Management perspectives, with perhaps more energy in Family. The perspective where the core cluster of values concentrates is our "home" perspective, which provides us with a general frame for how we see and understand things. Once a primary perspective of attention and energy has been established, the perspectives that are more oriented toward stability operate as our Foundation. For example, if our core perspective is Management, then the Grounding and Family perspectives generally operate together as a Foundational cluster. Similarly, in this example, the perspectives that are more characterized by valuing dynamism (Relational, Systems, and Expansion) would operate as our Vision cluster. The Foundation, Focus and Vision clusters must also overlap to some degree to maintain a correspondence between them and provide a person access to each cluster when needed.

Let's return to the perspectives model, presented in a generalized, linear fashion, with the Foundation, Focus, and Vision clusters superimposed on it:

Greater Stability *Greater Dynamism*

Foundation		Focus		Vision	
Grounding	**Family**	**Management**	**Relational**	**Systems**	**Expansion**
Surviving, and fulfilling the most basic needs. This is our most fundamental view toward the world, and is necessary for a solid life foundation.	Values in this perspective reflect kinship and social affiliation, and our most basic relationship to self and others.	These values are necessary for establishing and maintaining stability, and influencing within hierarchal contexts.	These values emphasize individual responsibility for developing one's own potential, as well as the quality of one's relationships with others.	These values address our interaction within dynamic groups, networks and larger systems, and influencing beyond our individual scope.	Values in this perspective act as guides to the future, our goals and aspirations. These values "pull" us toward globally-oriented vision.

Narrower Focus *Broader Focus*

Fig. 15 — Foundation, Focus and Vision Clusters

We have observed that the above continuum does suggest a left-to-right bias, showing an increasing degree of dynamism as well as an increasing degree of the scope of attention on the part of those who select the various perspectives. We have already discussed the problems associated with the stage-model, which leads to a reductive, "higher-better" default, with Foundation at the left and Vision at the right, which leaves Focus somewhere in the middle, and still implies a suggestion or an assumption that one should be moving toward the right.

But, we have observed a different set of relationships in operation among the perspectives, one that can be described by the work of Charles Hampton-Turner, who suggests a model that allows us to visualize the continuum in a more dynamic and generative manner. His model, in effect, bends the continuum so that the opposing ends are positioned as 90° axes.[76] If we bend the imaginary Foundation-Focus-Vision continuum at a 90° angle, then label the x and y axes Foundation and Vision, we get another way of looking at how these value clusters interact.

76 Charles Hampton-Turner, *Charting The Corporate Mind* (New York: The Free Press, 1990), 19-21.

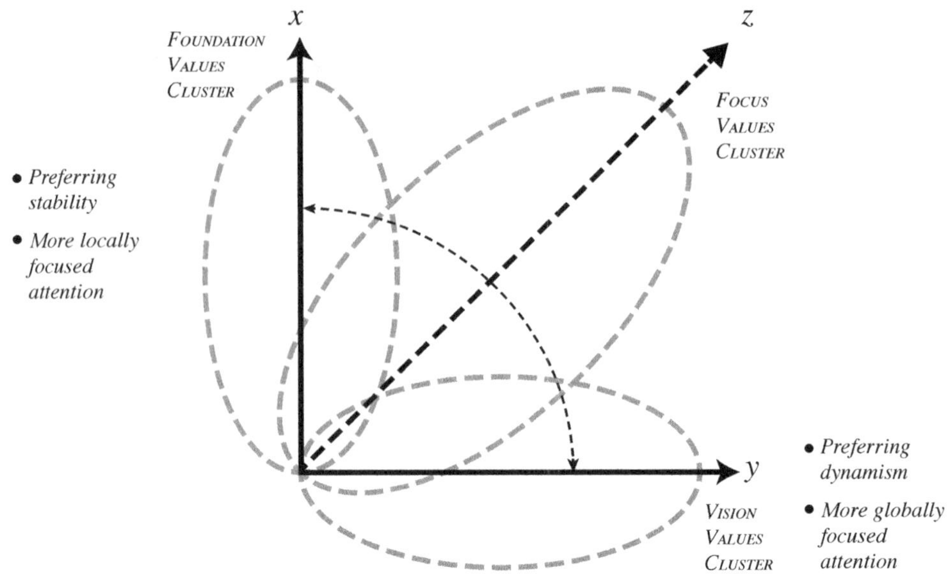

Fig. 16 — Interaction of Foundation, Focus and Vision Values Clusters

Using Hampton-Turner's representation frees us from the oppositional continuum model, with its implication that we may be more (or, less) of something (i.e., preferring greater stability vs. preferring greater dynamism; or narrowing our scope of attention vs. enlarging it), and instead gives us a different way of conceptualizing how the Foundation, Focus and Vision clusters may interact. Hampton-Turner points out that when we conceptualize a continuum, we tend to think of the opposite ends, as in fact, oppositional. We have to be, or value, one or the other.

In fact, any individual may be required at times to be able to activate values in situations that demand stability (i.e., more Foundational); and at other times, be able to activate taking a larger view, that allows for greater dynamism (i.e., more Visionary). Thus, the Focus values cluster may, for many people, in effect oscillate between these divergent demands. Further, in this representation, the Focus values are *not* meant to be understood as a synthesis of those two other clusters; instead the values in the Focus cluster are to be seen as linking across the model between the Foundation and Vision clusters. If this does not occur, then a person or group will find the Vision will not be realized, and when stresses or situations develop that trigger the need for Foundation values and skills, those will not be available to provide much needed support. Further, in a healthy values system, characterized by adequate reach, Foundation and Vision values are being revisited as needed.

When we depict the clusters in this way, we can see that the Focus cluster occupies a space that is in tension between the "pull" exerted by both the Foundation and Future values clusters, and it points a third direction that is between their axes. This begins to suggest a more accurate view of our focus of attention as a kind of pathway that oscillates between poles in tension. Our energy may be identified by an area we call Focus, but it is not as stable as we might assume. Situational influences are constantly at play and require us to place our awareness on values that are not in that designated area, so our energy may shift toward our Foundation or our Vision, and back again. Normally, that shifting is cyclical, but in real life, at least for most of us, those cycles are not regular and at times can seem randomly spontaneous. Hence, these graphic representations are suggestions to be understood metaphorically, not as rigid descriptions with mathematical precision. In short, the reality of values dynamics is complex, if not downright messy.

The spiral in the figure below is a representation of the process of development. Growth can indeed be seen as a progression. However, as we have iterated and reiterated, this progression is not fated to lead inevitably toward the "higher" Vision values. Instead, growth leads to a newly defined Focus. The z axis may tilt toward the Foundation (x) axis at any stage of life; or toward the Vision (y). Our development is always in essence an interaction between these three value clusters.

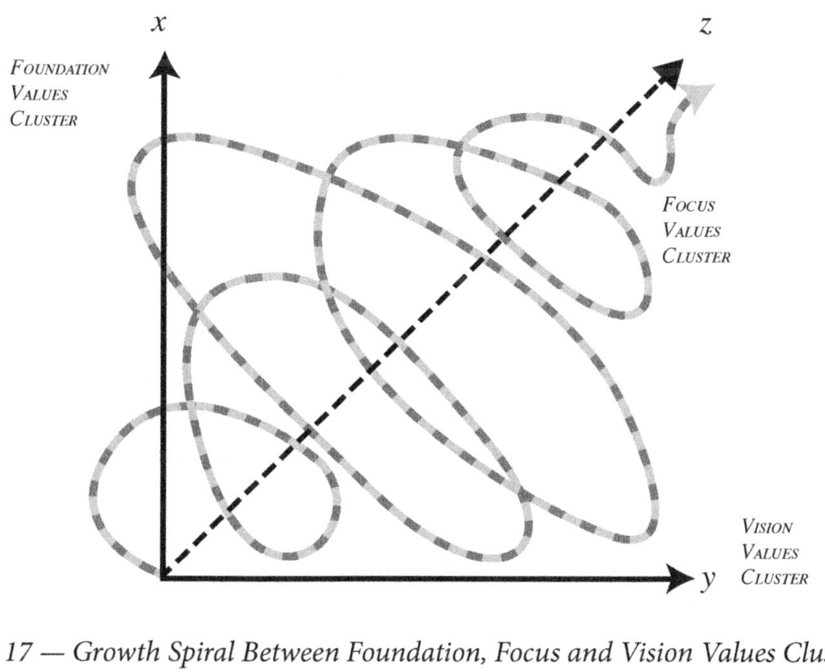

Fig. 17 — Growth Spiral Between Foundation, Focus and Vision Values Clusters

Learning occurs cyclically, not in a linear way. Educator and learning expert, Bernice McCarthy, has researched a four-part cycle for effective learning, based on work originally developed by David Kolb and Ron Fry in the 1970s at Case Western Reserve University. Each person has a predominant aspect, or penchant for a certain type of learning, but all people must experience the entire cycle for effective and complete learning to occur. Each step requires the stimulation of both left and right brain functioning. The steps are: 1) connection to the subject on a personal level, 2) factual and conceptual explanation, theory, and model-building, 3) practice and individual application, and 4) refinement and evaluation.[77]

We suggest that this kind of cycle occurs in values development. The function of the learning cycle is to extend our perception, triggering our awareness of values at the growing and lagging edges of our core focus. This function is not strictly contained within our Core Perspective, but can encompass values in contiguous views on both sides. Additionally, learning cycles may occur at the cluster level as identified above, where occasionally we temporarily move into our Foundation or Vision cluster as the occasion may demand of us.

Learning does not require that we must shift one perspective to the next in order, even though some of the values of one perspective do—at least conceptually—support the next. One might, for example jump from a Management core perspective where our attention and energy is focused, to a Systems core perspective because of professional demands; for example, a significant promotion might easily require this. And when a shift of this nature is required of us, we often are thrust into learning new skills associated with the values in the new perspective. However, in this case, the perspective that separates the two perspectives involved is Relational. We suggest that unless there are some values operating in this perspective to act as a functional bridge, in a supportive manner, that person's effectiveness and learning ability will be limited, and perhaps flawed. In other words, the third and fourth steps of the learning cycle, practice and refinement, both of which are necessary for competence, must have occurred in order for values to be supported by skills and behaviors. In our own work, we often encounter people who occupy senior leadership positions, but have never developed either the self-awareness or relational

77 Bernice McCarthy and Clif St. Germain, *The 4MAT Research Guide: Reviews of Literature on Individual Differences and Hemispheric Specialization and their Influence on Learning*. (Barrington, IL: Excel, Inc., 1996), 22-31. See also About Learning, "What is 4MAT?" accessed December 12, 2013, http://www.aboutlearning.com/what-is-4mat.

skills needed to be truly effective when working at a systems level. This becomes evident when they receive "360-degree" behavioral feedback from those around them, but without an understanding of the values dynamics involved, they are just as often confused as perhaps frustrated when they receive such feedback.

The following graphic represents what the relationship of value clusters might look like for a person with a core in Management perspective, who has also selected some significant priority values in Family, but has not selected many Relational values:

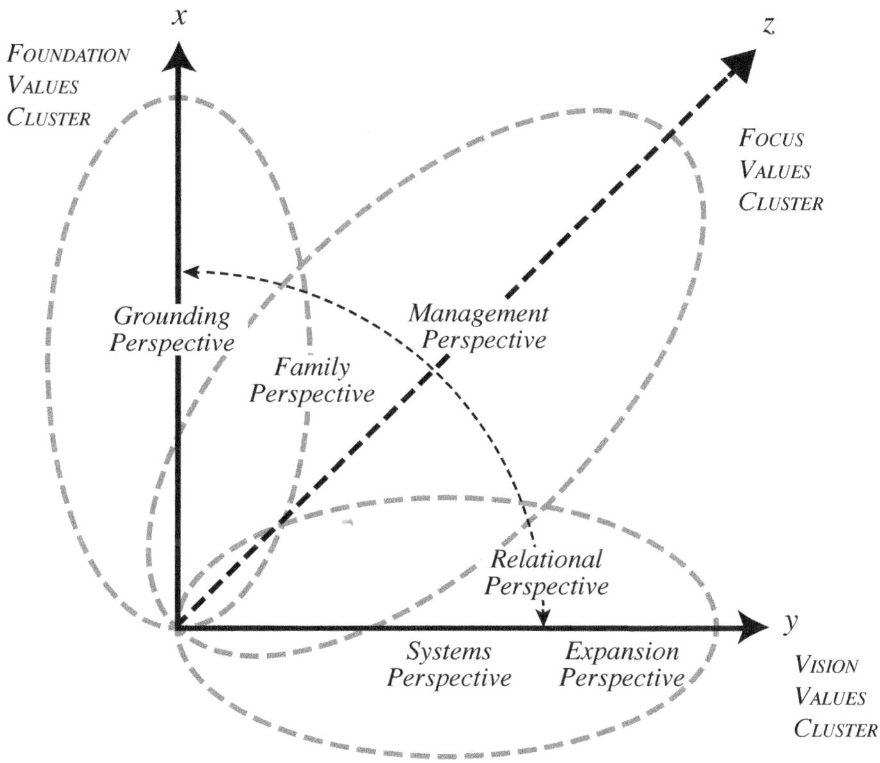

Fig. 18 — Example of Foundation, Focus and Vision Clustering

When talking with this person simply using the concept of clusters, we might start asking questions about the importance of stability (the Grounding, Family and Management perspectives are characterized by a preference for stability), to ascertain if that is indeed a behavioral strength, and how it plays out in daily life, at work, or otherwise. And then ask questions about the way relational priorities operate. A working hypothesis might be that the Family/Management perspective values are relatively well supported; that the Systems values may be operating as goals and aspirations; and that the Relational perspective is where attention might need to be given, to extend the individual's effective reach toward Vision cluster values. Only the individual can confirm this hypothesis. But, the model provides a place to start understanding how to approach a values-based, and eventually, a developmental conversation.

At the group level, growth can be suggested with an analogous process, but in a healthy group, actual individuals participate as representatives of the various clusters. That is, there will be some people that act as foundational and others as visionary, and at times their active participation—interjecting topics that address foundation, focus, and vision—is essential for group development. Their role does not necessarily mean their personal core perspective must be Grounding or Family (for Foundation), nor Systems or Expansion (for Vision), only that they be able to represent those perspectives. Without a clear understanding of how group development occurs, their participation might be seen as being irrelevant or counter to the group's Focus objectives, but indeed, we have seen many times, that without that sort of representation and an active group awareness and acknowledgement of its utility and importance, the group will not be able to either develop or be flexible enough to hold the space that is required for either remaining stable in the midst of chaotic change, or be able to listen and accept creative and innovative ideas.

We know of at least one large organization, an international corporation, founded and headquartered in Europe, which has determined how to put the notion of Foundation/Focus/Vision value clusters into practice.[78] This is a technology company, spanning a broad spectrum of technology fields and solutions, and as such, requires constant and deep innovation. Its leadership has mandated "intrapreneurship," meaning, that the company seeks to secure innovation talent within its ranks to develop new ideas and technologies. In practice, the notions of "secure" and "innovation" do not sit well together. Recognizing that ideators tend to have scant liking for the hierarchal structure that is common to corporate institutions and very often find themselves marginalized or simply leave for greener pastures, the company envisioned what might best motivate such talent to remain engaged, and thereby retain its best source of innovation. One

78 Christian Kurtzke, "Barriers and Enablers to Business Transformation towards the Knowledge Economy" (paper presented at the European Foundation for Management Development Special Event "Does Learning Pay?" Chipping Norton, England, September 27-29, 1998).

scheme involves identifying potential innovation projects, and soliciting applications from within the organization to lead such efforts, offering accompanying perquisites such as release from other job assignments, the ability to work distantly for the duration of a project, the assignment of dedicated staff, and flexible compensation and the guarantee of continued employment at the end of their involvement with a given project. This group in effect would become the Vision cluster of the organization. Recognizing, too, that existing strategic business units and the processes required to keep them running needed to be maintained, the company also recognized that existing roles and their supporting structures were necessary to the continued existence of the company. This would require re-asserting the value the company placed in its Foundation cluster. Finally, the company understood that many people in the organization would be required to function as bridgers between the interests and requirements for stability on the part of the Foundational functions, and the need to manage and resource the dynamic energy of the Vision project leaders and teams. Certain roles would be redesigned and would become key to assuring that intrepreneurs received the resources they needed, and translating those needs into terms acceptable with regard to standing policies and procedures; or influencing needed changes or exceptions. The company figured out the need for all three clusters, and resolved to appropriately support each, in effect, valuing each equally and treating each equally according to its characteristics and necessary contribution to continued success.

Values and Behavior

Values are the motivation for behavior. To use a metaphor, they are the gasoline that drives the engine. We may use the verbal symbols, the words that refer to particular values, but unless we have not only the behaviors, but also the behavioral skill level needed to accomplish or put a particular value into operation, the value remains an aspiration or a goal, at best. And if we claim proficiency in regard to a particular value and do not exhibit supporting behaviors, we will be quickly identified by others as not "walking the talk," which will erode our credibility, no matter if we are aware of it or not.

So values development is only partially a function of our priorities; it is also a function of learning the skills and competencies needed to place any particular value into operation. It is most likely that for our highest priority Focus values, we do have those skills and competencies, and at the same time, for every person, there are behaviors associated with any given value which we are either not familiar with, or cannot implement well enough for our purposes. This sort of development may, and often does, involve training in one way or another.

The link between values and behavior is an ancient recognition, but one about which there is still not clear or complete agreement. As you work with values, either your own or with others, you will need an understanding about this important relationship if any of this is to find an appropriate application in your lives. Consider this section a note on the important distinction between values and behavior.

What we value (i.e., where we place our attention) and how we behave may align, but they are two different things. If we don't have the skills to support a newly prioritized value, we may realize we are looking at a developmental need, and if feasible, may take steps to address it. A logical process of development occurs when we have sufficient skills to support our current core perspective, and begin to shift focus toward values found in other perspectives, but that we have not yet either worked with as priority values, or that we have skills to support. This is often in a perspective that is contiguous to our personal core perspective, but it is not limited to those areas.

Importantly, assessment of behaviors and skills is different from measuring values. When you respond to a survey that is based on your choices, you are measuring conscious priorities, i.e., what you value. If, in that assessment process we can discover a pattern or predominance in those choices, we can begin to say, "Your major focus of priorities, and therefore your attention, is in this perspective, and with this group of values." It makes sense to infer that behavior follows the choice of values. It often does, but by no means does it necessarily follow, a condition that can occur for a variety of reasons. Even when behavior does follow a value, there can be many different ways in which a value is behaviorally expressed and each of those possible behaviors has a latitude of competence to it. That is, each of us is more or less skilled at any of those behaviors.

This should not be understood as a problem, but it does present a caution. While it is quite possible to have a discussion about what behaviors represent a given value in a particular context, it is very difficult and therefore risky to do the opposite, that is, to observe a behavior and immediately assume it represents a specific value or lack of one. When we observe the world, we use our own core perspective as a frame through which we select information. The prism graphic below simplistically represents how a single value of "Responsibility" might easily be shown in a spectrum of behaviors, but as an observer, I might only be looking for one or two types of behaviors that correspond to my personal values perspectives, and therefore misunderstand, misinterpret or miss entirely, other behaviors which for the person doing the behaving, represent Responsibility perfectly and clearly.

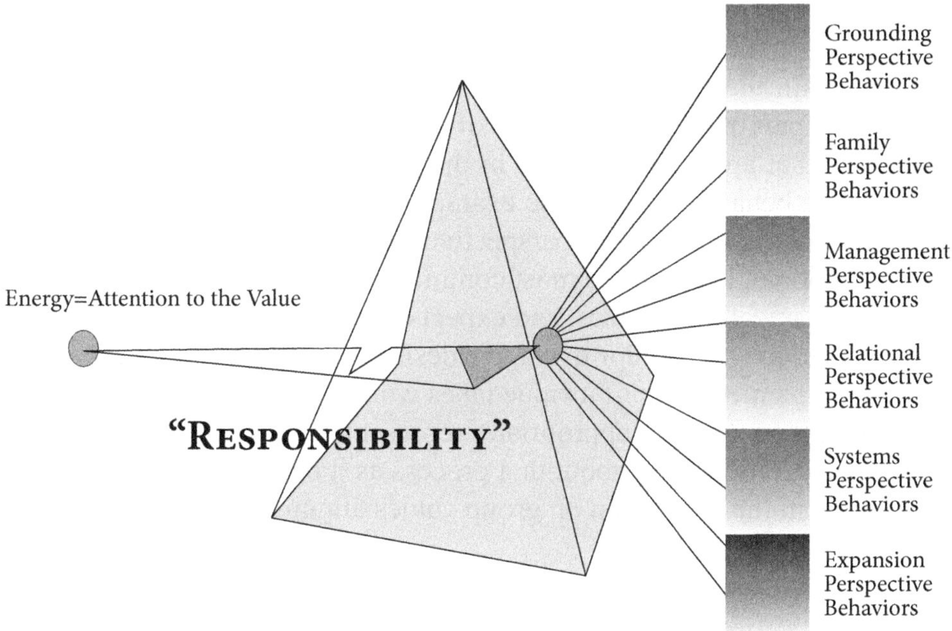

Fig. 19 — Values and Behaviors

We can espouse any values we like. Supporting that declaration with behavior is an entirely different matter. Conversely, it is also quite possible for us to perform in ways that are not supported by our own values. This can, of course, create an immediate sense of dilemma or anxiety if the difference between what we actually hold as values is greatly different from what we are required to do. At the minimum, it may require an expense of energy corresponding to the degree of tension between what we value and what the situation demands of us. The point is that behavior does not always follow obvious, personal values, so we must be careful in making the distinction between values and development. Furthermore, since behavior is extremely susceptible to situational influences, we must also be careful not to ascribe a particular value as the root or basis for a behavior without some additional supporting evidence.

Then how do we deal with the value-behavior question in actual situations, at work for example? The answer is simple, but its execution may take some effort: talk about it. This is what the "Alignment" process is all about. It takes a discussion to answer the question, "What does a particular value look like for us?" The most functional answer is a set of a few representative behaviors. One particular company we have worked with has, like many organizations, significant administrative, plant and field operations. So they were careful to gather examples for their company values taken from the field, and from the office. Another company, a large civil engineering and construction firm, has published together with their values representative behaviors as examples (3-4 per value) as a part of their ethical code of conduct. Interestingly, many of the examples that apply to those out in the field are Grounding and Family perspective behaviors, and those examples that come from a supervisory orientation are Management perspective behaviors. But these companies are exceptional, because the most common approach is to simply publish a set of organizational values, and expect employee behavior to appear, as if by magic, in ways senior managers desire.

The implementation of a value takes work. Work to really understand the value, then practice appropriate, representative behaviors over time, and if in a group, to talk about that process as it occurs. We have more to add to this in the discussion on group values alignment found in Part V.

Part V:
The Values Practitioner

This section is about basic values practice. In it, we will discuss basic guidelines for working with values at three levels of application: individual values development; how values operate between individuals in relationship with others; and values alignment in groups and organizations. Because The Values Perspective posits that values work begins on the personal level, and that the values one holds are not determinative of one's level of emotional, cognitive or moral development, it is important to conduct values work from the standpoint of discovery. That means that the identification and, if desired, re-ordering or addition to, a values set is always under the control of the person or group engaging in values work. In short, as adults, each individual is in charge of one's values and associated behaviors.

We have said that working with values requires a context of safety and respect, in which participants may talk about values without worrying that what they say or what they choose to keep private will be negatively judged, especially at work. Our understanding of safety includes its physical, psychological, and social aspects. In a safe environment, candid comments can be made, questions will be heard, and deepened dialogue may follow that will clarify what a person's values mean, or what similarities or differences between individuals' or groups' values sets mean for the group. This kind of discussion provides an understanding of the basic dynamics of how values operate in a person's life, and can provide an objective and neutral structure for setting the stage for a coaching conversation, or at a group level, an intervention or alignment. At the same time, as with any discovery or developmental opportunity, theory and model are used largely to posit hypotheses and validate or invalidate them through a structured engagement. Too much theory introduced into a coaching or consulting session can be counter-productive because it may deflect attention away from actual behavioral applications. Goals, intentions and desired outcomes are always important, and ultimately provide a guide for how a values discussion is conducted.

Ethics and Values

Values drive behavior. This is well established. The Values Perspective is careful—as much as possible—to not introduce judgments regarding what should be done with one's values, what one's values should be or what behaviors necessarily follow from a particular value. That is the domain of ethics. Ethics prescribe what behavior is considered to be acceptable and preferred. Ethics are necessarily bound to a specific context, usually social or cultural, and inform a code of conduct. Many times, for example in organizations, this code is made explicit, published, and employees or other members are asked to pledge to behave in support of it, or lose membership in that group. All of that is appropriate and necessary.

The Values Perspective model and assessment survey helps facilitate discussions of ethics, but is not in itself an assessment of what is ethical. The Values Perspective is designed to be used by people from different countries and cultures, who represent any industry or sector whether education, government, healthcare, and other not-for-profit organizations, or as single individuals. The model and survey results simply provide a systematic identification of what is important for an individual or group.

The discussion of what is ethical in regard to one's values, or in regard to a group's values, is the next step after the identification of what values are actually in operation. The Values Perspective model, survey, and subsequent reports are useful tools for discussions regarding what an ethical code consists of, what parts of that code are being supported, and what parts may need attention. But the Values Perspective does not indicate how decisions should be made in regard to the ethical dilemmas, which often require compromises and tradeoffs of values priorities that we all encounter from time to time. This requires discussion, and an individual's or group's set of highly-prioritized values act as a guideline for discussion and decision-making.

Values Are Our Strengths

As we have discussed previously, values are energy, and that energy shows up in our language and behavior. We commonly attribute our motivations to our highest priorities, or what are often referred to as our strengths. They are what seem natural for us as individuals. In our consulting work, we ascribe to a strengths-based approach to working with values, which is based on our fundamental assertion that no value is a priori better or more desirable than any other. We, therefore, do not promote any value or any values perspective as something an individual or group *should* espouse.

When we speak of values as energy and strengths, this means that values represent energy that drives decisions and has a tendency to draw people holding similar values toward each other. Because values are energetic, it also means that selecting a new value may require a conscious expenditure of energy to keep it prioritized for a sufficient length of time to identify and seek to develop the skills needed to operationalize it as desired. In this way, values may lead to strengths that others can see.

We know from our own practice that having a set of strengths does not necessarily mean that a person is able to maximize that set of strengths behaviorally. However, having a strength does mean that attention and energy are present to motivate skill acquisition. In a similar way, values are motivators. Because values are motivators, we can suggest that *any value in the values field may be selected as suitable to serve a particular goal.* People are often very creative about how they successfully apply their values. At the same time, an individual or group will be best served in selecting a set of values that, in the best judgment of the individual or group, will focus their energy toward the desired outcome. A values set comprises whatever an individual or group recognizes as valuable as identified through reflection, dialogue or a survey, plus whatever additional values they may consciously choose to adopt, for whatever reason. What makes a value choice desirable is a person's or a group's available and aspirational energy, as expressed by their values, with regard to their situation, needs, goals and aspirations. As coaches or consultants, we may contribute our own hypotheses or suggestions as to which value or values may serve the purpose at hand. But, the values always belong to the individual or group, and must reflect a snapshot in which they may recognize what they really value, as well as what is within reach with regard to what they might aspire toward and by "reach" we mean the ability to value across the spectrum of values perspectives. This picture is different in every case.

We have observed that values can cluster into mutually supportive tracks, and an individual or group may determine that a particular value can be viewed as a sort of keystone around which other values may naturally cluster. What those particular values are has to make sense to the individual or the group, and the goal of a coach or facilitator is to aid this sense-making process. Generally, a keystone value is one that an individual or group validates as important, and that already has a high priority within their values set. A process may then begin of looking to surrounding perspectives, for more foundational values that support the keystone value; and more future-oriented values that look toward the natural aspirational outcomes envisioned by the individual or group as important.

Part of the work we do with the Values Perspective reports is to provide a summary of a person's values selections as they are distributed across the various perspectives. Such a summary can quickly be understood as a sort of energy map. Individual data can be seen the same way in aggregate form for a group, to suggest where the energy of the group is being directed in terms of priorities. The presentations of these summaries always lead to interesting questions, "Are these really our strengths?" And lively discussions that follow can be extremely productive.

Asking Questions

When coaching individuals, or working with values in teams or groups, our objective is to help them to discover their values, and to use this conscious understanding to aid them with life, work and legacy. The values process always involves asking questions. Questions may be used by a coach or consultant to test hypotheses, to help an individual or group to define values and recognize values language and behaviors, and to set intentions for development.

Our general approach is:

- Start with strengths
    - ◊ What are the highest-priority values? Why?
    - ◊ Does the priority-order describe you? How?
    - ◊ How do these values show up? What do they mean in your life or work?
    - ◊ How do you define these values? How do you 'live' them?

  - ◊ What behaviors are in place to operationalize them?
  - ◊ Is anything missing? Is there a value or values important in your life or work that you need to add?

- Look for support
  - ◊ What skills might be sought to operationalize or strengthen high-priority values that are more aspirational, and may need strengthening behaviorally?
  - ◊ What other values or behaviors might be needed to support your aspirations with regard to these values? (They might be more Foundational, they might be additional Focus values, or they might be Vision values)
  - ◊ Are there people you can enlist to help with information, support (emotional or logistical) and/or ideas or informed perspectives?

- Identify one or two goals for development
  - ◊ What changes might you like to make, with regard to your highest priorities?
  - ◊ What steps do you need to take to realize these priorities?
  - ◊ How will you undertake achieving the changes you want to make?
  - ◊ How will you judge or measure your progress? Whom do you want to partner with who will help you be accountable to your intentions and goals?

Working with Definitions

The definitions of the values offered in The Value Perspectives survey are intentionally generic and as succinct as possible. This is done to allow each person or group to start with a basic definition and make necessary adjustments to allow it to accurately represent the value in question. This is a pragmatic approach, which allows the Values Perspective to be used in any cultural or organizational context or situation. We know from our experience that people will always tend to add their own meaning to the definitions of values in any case. It is simply human nature.

What is often most helpful for people, in regard to refining the definitions for their values is to identify 3 or 4 representative behavioral examples for each of their highest priority values. This accomplishes a couple of things at the same time. First, it provides tangible referents for the abstract value name, and second, people usually find that the refinements are not changes in the definition, but are situational needs. That is, they find that a given value is triggered by the need to behave in a particular way in a particular situation. This makes understanding the value easier and makes the definition richer in meaning, while the essence of the definition is retained.

It is the nature of each values perspective to provide a structural orientation, such that we will tend to define a given value through the lens of that perspective. For example, the value of legacy may mean something different to a person who holds a core Family perspective (e.g., providing for offspring's inheritance, or a desire to be remembered by family) than for someone holding a core Systems perspective (e.g., being published, or being recognized as a theorist in an inter-disciplinary domain). We reveal our values, and generally, the perspective that serves as the lens through which we are viewing the world through the language we use. A skilled coach or facilitator will recognize perspective cues and be able to mirror back those cues as appropriate to a person or group. This is particularly important to observe in relationship coaching or intervention, and in group or organizational values consulting. Recognizing that perspective and other factors may influence how the same value is defined differently leads to the difference between "That's not how I define it" and "Now I understand why it is we seem to disagree."

Communication and Values

Shared values often result in the development of a relationship, whether that relationship is between individuals, an individual and a group, or an individual and a concept, like a philosophy, religion, or political orientation. Sharing values often facilitates sharing information, but that alone is not human communication. The most simple and profound definition of human communication, and likely one of the most accurate, is simply "shared understanding between two or more people." However, this definition is a little misleading. The concept of communication has been plagued with a mechanical model of Sender-Message-Medium-Receiver-Interpretation for nearly a century. Humans are complex and subtle, and so is the communication that occurs between them. However, it is human nature to assume a shared understanding based on shared values. Likewise, we find it much more difficult to find the way to shared understanding when our values are significantly different. Everyone has experienced the difficulties arising from this.

Even if people share the same perspective and share the same value, miscommunication is still a risk if they do not take the time to talk about what that value means, how each person thinks it works for him or her, and what they expect of the other person or people. The next step is to take the time to agree about those issues.

When people who hold different perspectives communicate, they often share fewer common experiences to refer to when a dialogue occurs, so even if they are using the same words, their interpretations of those words will be different. We all tend to internally re-define each value based on our perspective, personality, individual background, and present situations. For this reason, a dialogue between two people holding different perspectives must be given the time needed to delve into those definitions and share enough of the experiences they are based on to become mutually intelligible. This can then become the basis for mutual understanding.

Overall, when people share a values perspective communication is more likely simply because they are more likely to find themselves in both formal and informal discussions which provide lots of opportunities for both sharing and clarifying. When people do the same thing, but whose core perspectives are 'adjacent' to each other, the opportunities for informal discussions decrease and communication problems begin to appear more frequently. For people whose core perspectives are not contiguous (i.e., there is a gap between them), the likelihood of miscommunication becomes likely because not only do they not share common referents, but they will have experienced the same event differently enough so that their interpretation might easily sound like two different events, and unless they have received some communication training, they might easily avoid each other, lacking both the energetic connection of shared values and perhaps the skill, motivation, or patience needed to create a bridge across the gulf.

Often, it has been assumed that it is somehow the responsibility of a person holding what has been seen as a higher values perspective to reach 'down' to aid the understanding of a person holding a lower perspective. We could write another book simply debunking this myth. Learning to, literally, value the perspective of another person involves expanding one's reach across the values spectrum, from whatever core perspective position on the values field one may occupy. Frequently, the most effective partnerships are between individuals or groups holding differing core perspectives, who learn how to communicate with each other. This is accomplished initially by using the values language of the perspective one wishes to influence, or to create a bridge of communication with.

We cannot stress strongly enough the need for basic, intentional communication skills training. Values are energy, and when mixed into an interpersonal or set of group relationships, communication attempts can immediately become emotionally charged. Appropriate communication training can supply the needed skills to maintain communication, even across values gaps.

Values At Work

Since the mid-1950s, authors have been discussing leadership, teams, and organizations and their development with the familiar terminology of "levels of observation."[79] "Individual," "team," and "organization" are terms that describe specific contextual identifications, and which serve to focus our attention at a given level of interaction and transaction. Language is powerful, and has a profound impact on the way we understand everything around us. What we get from these terms is an intervention structure, which functionally amounts to a schema with which to diagnose and attend to problems. The problem is that we impose these static terms on organizations, thinking we are actually describing them when we are not. A different set of terms would allow us to both describe and intervene more appropriately into a system. Finally, different terms will remind us that organizational systems are fundamentally composed of people, as interacting participants, in varying sets of relationships, including relationship to self.

The terms we prefer to use are *individual*, *relationship*, and *alignment*. We think of them as interdependent, and in practice they and their associated processes are iterative. They build one upon the other, not in a straight linear way, but in a sort of triad of concepts that support the organizing process, and allow for it to result in stable and/or dynamic results, that is to say, to recognize the need to move at any given time more Foundationally or in a more Vision-oriented direction, or both, to achieve optimal reach. Thus, we may not develop a straight hierarchy with these three terms as is possible with the terms "individual, team, organization," nevertheless, if we think of these in terms as three points in a cycle, we may understand that the interaction of values and complexity is emergent and that these three terms comprise a model with which we may understand how we all develop and work with others in the organizations within which we live.

---

79 Stephen W. Littlejohn, *Theories of Human Communication,* 1st ed. (Columbus, OH: Merrill, 1978), 4.

The Individual Level

At the individual level, values work is always about self-actualization, but not exactly in the sense that Maslow made the term famous. Maslow felt only a small number of people could achieve self-actualization, which is the fulfilling of one's full potential. We see self-actualization as a process, and not an achievement. When seen in this way, self-actualization can more easily be defined as available to each person, without prejudice with regard to what a person's level of development might be judged to be, by any number of criteria. It is incumbent on each of us to discover what it means for us to develop our own talents and address our limitations. In this sense, no matter what the general focus stage or core perspective one may hold, each person can engage in his or her own self-actualization process. We often refer to this process as "Leadership with a small l," meaning that leadership starts with leading one's self toward full potential. The research done by Don Clifton, and the positive psychology movement in general, indicates the remarkable energy and ability that we tap when we use our native talents and strengths.[80] It is noteworthy that many of the concepts identified as "strengths" in the positive psychology literature and assessment instruments are identical to values found in many values assessment surveys as well.

Where an individual finds him- or herself in the context of the values field (see Fig. 12, above) can be predictive of the challenges he or she will encounter in life and at work. People whose core perspective is Family or Management may find themselves challenged when presented with the need to manage in rapidly changing and ambiguous situations. More importantly, as an individual finds him- or herself in increasingly dynamic situations he or she must be able to accommodate that dynamism and ambiguity without being personally threatened. If one's self esteem (self-worth is a Family perspective value), is threatened, one is thrown into a defensive posture, and is unable to do much except maintain one's psychological security, much less lead others in complex environments. Though the values core perspective may suggest this or other issues as potential challenges, breaking out of this condition is by no means impossible. It requires attention and conscious expenditure of energy toward identifying and acquiring the skills to surpass limiting factors. This will involve a re-prioritizing of values, and/or the adoption of a value

80 Marcus Buckingham and Donald O. Clifton, *Now, Discover Your Strengths* (New York: The Free Press, 2001).

or values that will direct attention accordingly. A strong sense of self-worth can be built based on one's own personal preferences and strengths. Likewise, people whose core perspective is Systems may be challenged in situations or domains where maintenance or stability is required. The challenge here may be one involving the cultivation of respect (a Family perspective value) such that others in the environment may recognize that they are being respected, according to their own definition. Recognizing that strongly held values operate as biases for all of us allows an individual to understand and manage his or her own biases, leverage strengths, and look for opportunities to establish partnerships to accomplish objectives for which others may have greater talent or expertise.

The challenge is more than providing a helping hand so a person can identify native strengths and talents. Those talents must be directed toward productive application or frustration will result. Underdeveloped areas, even if they fall in a category of natural talent, must be addressed and developed. And since we are all called on to function in ways where natural talent and strengths are not sufficient to achieve results, those areas must be managed developmentally.

The "Individual" orientation emphasizes individual responsibility and control for development both personally and professionally, which is consistent with the emerging view, particularly in the corporate environment, that each person must manage one's own career. In addition, there is a great deal of work that positively correlates the active engagement or participation of people in organizations with productivity, profit, safety, retention, etc.[81] When people are confirmed in terms of their own values and contributions, they are immediately engaged, and although there may be many ways to achieve that development, use of values theory is one powerful and highly effective way to do that.

However, individual development raises some challenges. It is appropriate to reiterate that development is not a one-way, linear progression through the various values perspectives we have outlined in this book. The first challenge we face at the individual level is to first make sure our Foundation, Core, and Vision values clusters are supported with skills. Second, the next challenge is to examine one's own core perspective and ask if there are values that need our attention, which we have ignored. Third, we

---

81 See the work of Marcus Buckingham and Curt Coffman, First Break All The Rules, New York: Simon and Schuster. 1999; also, Daniel Denison, *Corporate Culture and Organizational Effectiveness*, New York: John Wiley & Sons, 1990), and Stanley A. Deetz, Sarah J.. Tracy, S., and Jennifer L. Simpson, *Leading Organizations through Transitions: Communication and Cultural Change* (Thousand Oaks, CA: Sage, 2000).

look to perspectives adjunct to our core, and examine the supporting links between values that exist between the perspectives.

Finally, once a person receives some insight about his or her self, particularly in terms of values, then it is natural for sharing and comparisons to begin. The recognition of those differences is important, because that recognition immediately surfaces a need to manage the differences that become obvious when the individual simply looks around at others in any given group. Hence, the second phase of the model is the need and development of relationship skills to manage those differences. It is worth noting in all of this review of individual development that moving one's core perspective emphasis has not been included. That sort of change does occur as a part of some people's development, but it is not a necessary requirement for all people. What, instead, we may regard as a requirement is to be able to sufficiently extend our reach into other values perspectives in order to strengthen our own values set and enable us to communicate with, influence and work with people whose core perspectives differ from our own.

An Individual Values Development Example

Some years ago we were with an entire group of development consultants, coaches, and high level administrators—all colleagues working in the same institution who were all in the process of learning about and working with values assessment and development. A survey was administered as part of the process, and when it was passed out and explained, the natural thing began to happen. People began to compare their individual reports, but had misunderstood the results. The reports were interpreted as a sort of "score," where one core perspective was considered a step higher and somehow more advanced than a previous perspective. Given their choice of work, it was not surprising that most of the group shared either the Relational or Systems perspectives as their respective core perspective. Remarks were made that would not likely have been made in the presence of clients. There were several remarks that were troublesome as we knew everyone in the group fairly well, and understood that none of us had much room for bragging. One woman, Elizabeth, who was and remains a good friend and colleague of ours, was in the group, and was obviously quiet. We continued though the session, and then took a break for lunch. Both of us met Elizabeth in the hall; she was visibly upset. She felt as if the results had made her look somehow inferior. Her core perspective was Family. The comments made by others had clearly indicated that she was not as visionary as others. It was a momentary disaster.

What no one but the three of us in that room knew was that Elizabeth, who had just turned 40, had just learned she was pregnant for the first time. Of course, she and her husband were overjoyed, but what she didn't realize was that the recent news had precipitated a huge change in the focus of her values. While as a professional, she was as visionary as the best of them, as a prospective mother-to-be her core perspective was *exactly* where it should have been. The questions she was facing were all about the physical, emotional, and relational changes and challenges the pregnancy had immediately imposed on her. Her individual development challenges were not in any way less-than those of her colleagues, but they did come from a different perspective. The report had correctly identified where her attention and energy had shifted. When we sat together and explained this, it made sense to her, and she was able to validate it from her feelings and experience. In her case, what she had internalized as a judgment that her core was "regressive" in comparison to her colleagues, she was able to re-evaluate taking into account her life situation, which required re-building her Foundation. She was able to recognize, and redefine, this regression to rebuild a values Foundation as a constructive, developmental move. At this writing, she has two healthy, wonderful children. As a coach and consultant, her value is enhanced because of her experience and of her recognition of what it means to be compelled to re-visit Foundational values. For us, it was also a developmental experience, as it reified our understanding with regard to the powerful cultural bias that exists that "higher is better," and that this bias usually needs to be positively pre-empted when beginning values work at any level of intervention.

Values and Relationships

Relationships are the essence of organization. Humans are social, and being in relationship is a human condition. Being relational does not mean that we are necessarily skilled at relationship. Although we may succeed in forming personal relationships through elective affinity and sharing of values, and hopefully may develop over time the attitudes and skills we need to preserve those relationships of choice, we may lack the luxury of selecting whom we relate with at work.

Personally, we think of relationships in terms of significant others in our lives, spouses, children, friends, etc. Professionally, we think of our relationships within the primary group in which we work. Group relationships are the fundamental building blocks for getting work done in a collaborative way. And generally, the more complicated and sophisticated the work, the more we must depend on successful relationships with others.

In today's organizational environment, people often belong to multiple groups and teams, many of which have only temporary identities, and nearly continually changing memberships. Increasingly, those groups are geographically dispersed and at times totally virtual. People now commonly find themselves in matrix structures with multiple reporting relationships, have multiple co-worker relationships that cross functional as well as traditional hierarchical boundaries, are responsible for internal as well as external customer relationships which further blur group boundaries, and often are additionally responsible for achieving objectives with no direct authority in terms of relationship partners. This is not to say that in many organizations there are not stable and discrete teams and groups, for that is the case much of the time. One of the major challenges leaders face today is being responsible for creating a "high performing team" on a moment's notice, as if that accomplishment was a part of every successful leader's abilities. This not a reasonable expectation for several reasons, among which is the time and energy required to develop quality relationships. A common rule of thumb for team development is it takes 12 to 18 months to develop a group to the point of high performance.

Values Perspective theory indicates that people with significant differences in perspective are likely to experience communication and relationship problems *even if they share some of the same values.* People sharing the same perspective may assume that their relationship and communication is effective because they do not often encounter obvious relationship problems. If placed in a close working relationship and the stakes involve reputation for example, they may come to discover that similar language does not automatically mean that they actually define the values they share in the same way. When working closely together, they may come to discover that what they *mean* is more nuanced than what they *say*, and requires mutual unpacking.

Importantly, it is the quality of the relationship that allows for real differences to be managed. The Values Perspective theory and model can be used to surface differences in perspective and in how values are defined. And, it provides an objective structure that can be used to guide dialogue that explores assumptions, generates clarity and increases understanding, which in turn provides a sound foundation for building and maintaining relationships.

Typically, organizational careers are advanced through promotion into positions of wider scope. The need to expand reach into perspectives characterized by a wider scope can be a challenge in itself. The need to be able to reach toward others holding different perspectives will also increase as the difference in scope increases. Generally, effective managers are much more those who shift their priority toward acquiring a wide reach rather than those who choose to concentrate their efforts in maintaining highly developed technical or business skills. Even in the case where such skills are requisite to maintaining credibility with some constituents, highly skilled professionals may fail when promoted if they do not place a significant amount of energy toward cultivating reach. The critical quality that identifies the essence of organizations is the quality of the relationships that exist between those who are coordinating the various activities of people who form the system, and their ability to reach across the spectrum of perspectives represented in the organizational population. Of course, reach may be attained through teaming with people who have diverse core perspectives. This by definition still requires being able to value another perspective from the standpoint of one's own.

An Example of Values and Relationship

In the course of conducting a team building retreat aimed toward the values of collaboration and synergy, it became obvious that two of the participants had some underlying tension between them. During the workshop, we dealt with an incident when one of the two made a comment that implied feeling left out of the information loop, but wondered if the responses coming from the group that the information in question had been readily available, were going to be sufficient even though the retreat was said by participants to be successful. However, we soon received a call asking if we could facilitate a conflict resolution session between the two parties who had exchanged some strong statements during the workshop. We agreed, and conducted individual interviews with each party to assess what was going on.

As we conducted the individual, private interviews preceding the actual one-on-one dialogue, we found a difficult case. Some of the critical incidents the parties, Tom and Susan, cited as sources of their conflict were more than three years old. It was extremely obvious that the two had entirely different recollections of what had happened, so a simple resolution was not an option. What was also important was that Tom had a Management core perspective, while Susan had a Family core perspective. The difference in the language they used to describe what was important to them in this situation was a near perfect reflection of their larger, and differing, sets of values priorities.

It became very clear that the operational priorities for Tom, the Organization core perspective manager, were authority, critical thinking, and responsibility. Susan, the Family core Perspective manager, prioritized fairness, inclusion and respect. These are two very different sets of priorities. Probing for additional values, we did find that values they held in common were productivity and quality. In preparation for dialogue, we recommended each of them identify something about the other that was genuinely and positively notable if not appreciated, which could be expressed in a specific behavioral statement. We recommended that at some time during the conversation they each be prepared to share that statement.

The face-to-face session started with some significant, silent tension. After a short introduction during which we called out the values they held commonly, we were simply quiet, and the two managers took turns. We had established some interaction ground rules that we had to remind people about more than once. Finally each side had expressed his or her opinion and responded. We made sure that both parties felt they had been allowed to say what was important and had been able to respond to the other. The energy had calmed considerably, but neither had shared a positive statement about the other. A pause … then Tom, the Organizational perspective manager said, “I want you to know that in spite of our difficulties, I think you are a really good manager.” Up to that point, they had really just avoided running into each other. But he picked out the value of competence from his core perspective, which he attributed to Susan, and shared it honestly and respectfully. Of course Susan, the Family core perspective manager did not even recognize the statement as one reflective of competence as she viewed it, but Tom’s honesty and respect came through to her loud and clear. Both of these values reside in the Family Perspective. Susan immediately responded with thanks and seemed to relax for the first time. Some conversation ensued, but before long she reciprocated with asking his advice on a particular problem. Without even realizing it, she reciprocated his competence value in the form of a question.

The meeting ended shortly thereafter, everyone was pleased and not quite sure what had happened. It was certainly not what the two managers had feared or expected. The past had not been erased, nor was it even completely resolved. But what they accomplished was the beginning of a new working relationship between them, based on greater mutual respect.

Values in Alignment: The Group and Organizational Level

Alignment refers to people in a group or organization

- sharing the same values,
- in the same priority, and
- agreeing on at a set of representative behaviors associated with those values.

No matter that a purpose is shared, or that group members interact (or not). Indeed, when a purpose is shared, and people interact, but do not possess effective relationship skills, the result is often miscommunication and confusion, eventual mistrust and the failure of the leadership relationship. Without functional relationship skills, no organization can establish the necessary feedback loops to sustain itself in any modern context. Relationships are held together through an alignment process. This process is iterative. Once established, it needs to be revisited, and extended to new organizational members.

Alignment is also referred to as "perceived similarity," "the attraction paradigm," and "the attraction hypothesis." It is a standard psychological principle that has been well researched. "Perceived similarity is the degree to which we believe another's characteristics are similar to ours, is often sufficient to attract us to others."[82] It is achieved through a process of comparison and dialogue. Comparison allows for awareness of similarity or difference, and dialogue allows for the maintenance of similarity in relationships, and management of differences.

There is a basic principle that describes the way values work as a sort of "relationship glue:" *When a person sees his or her own values reflected in a group or organization, that person will automatically and immediately be drawn to engage in that organization.* However, since we know there will always be some differences in any relationship or group of relationships, to the degree those differences are not well managed, they become a repulsive force: *To the degree that one's personal values are not reflected by a group, a mutual repulsion begins to occur between the individual and the group.*

It is important to note that the reverse, "repulsion principle," has also been researched, and has been shown to be the more powerful of the two.[83]

---

82 Dominic Infante, Theodore Avtgis, and Andrew Rancer, *Contemporary Communication Theory* (Dubuque, IA: Kendall Hunt, 2010), 260.

83 R. Sing, Ho Yan Soo, "Attitudes and Attraction: A New Test of the Attraction,

If differences are not well managed, the individual will leave the group, or the group will expel the individual, or both.

Effective leaders recognize and take advantage of the above principles in coordinating individual efforts and managing the relationships between people in groups and teams. Even in relatively stable environments, these principles are strongly functional, but in dynamic, complex environments, where the system itself may be dramatically changing, they may determine whether organizational survival is probable or not because it is precisely in the diversity of the group where a robust potential exists.

Values alignment accounts for effective organization maintenance. However, there is much to be decided in regard to shared values, including their overall priority, and an understanding of acceptable behaviors that support those values. Without self-awareness and relationship skills, embarking on an alignment process often results in frustration, confusion, and many times failure. Hence, there is a general order to these concepts that goes far beyond a simple expansion in scope.

Traditionally, working at the "organizational level" generally involves concepts and skills described by terms like systems thinking, strategic planning, vision and mission statement development, structural reorganization (breaking down silos), value statements, succession plans, information management systems, customer relations, SWOT analyses (strengths, weaknesses, opportunities, threats), marketing strategy, innovation (research and development), etc. However, the dynamic nature of an organization as a system makes the task of actually dealing with it as an entity extremely difficult. Parts of organizations that span large geographic distances are often in partial operation through a 24-hour day, but never all at the same time. Individuals may be entering as new members or leaving the system at any time without the awareness of others. Currently, some parts of many organizations are virtual, doing business with automated processes via the Internet and indeed some organizations are totally virtual which provides a challenge in determining just exactly what and where the organization is at any given time. The point is that alignment within an organization is a continual process, which usually operates at a tacit level. At times, that process should be made explicit to keep the organization diverse and healthy in terms of the diversity of perceptions it contains.

Repulsion and Similarity-Dissimilarity Asymmetry Hypotheses," *British Journal of Social Psychology* 39, no. 2, (October, 2001), 197-211.

Attempting an organizational values intervention can be very demanding and even risky. It is much safer to work at the individual or team levels than working with the entire organization. Just consider that in any given organization there is always a certain percentage of disaffected people, people who are living the repulsion principle, but have not left the organization. We have heard the term "CAVE dwellers" used to describe them: Certainly Against Virtually Everything. And a values intervention can release a lot of pent up emotional energy from people who do not share the actual, functioning organizational values. Recognizing this, we do not recommend complete organizational values intervention without careful consideration with each organization, and without adequate proactive support for and from the organizational population.

Alignment is a functional approach to organizational intervention. "Alignment," does not supplant the term "organization," any more than the "relationship" supplants "team." Both old and new sets of terms function for different reasons. Nevertheless, it is a demanding approach, for as far as we understand, there is only one way to effect alignment, and that is through a process of dialogue. The essence of dialogue is the development of true consensus, on the explicit values, their operational definitions, including supporting examples, and their priority, that determine the Foundation, Focus, and Vision of the organization.

The requirement of dialog begs the question that leaders possess well developed skills that not merely allow for, but foster dialogue, conflict management, understanding and leveraging diversity, and developing the necessary basins of attraction that support collaborative interaction. These skills are profoundly important to the survival of dynamic systems, and are too easily thought of as "soft skills," as if they occupy a place of less importance in comparison to the more "hard skills" of technology and business.

It is not necessary for an individual manager to completely understand the nature, power, and function of language itself to successfully satisfy the dialogic requirement of the alignment process, but it helps. Suffice it to say that we live in and with language at such an intimate level that it becomes causal to our perceptions and our very identities. As we mentioned earlier, James Powell suggests that we have external and internal languages. The external language can be made explicit, and importantly, is socially regulated. Internal language provides us with opportunities to create, to hold self-dialogues, to reflect and to analyze in private. It is within this interior language that we are able to "break away from the fixed outer language."[84]

---

84 Powell, 35.

It is through the process of bringing internal values into external language through dialogue that alignment occurs. More than simply putting labels on intangible values, dialogue also provides the relationship structure for organizing and reorganizing to occur in the midst of chaos. Dialogue allows for the sharing, listening and trust to develop that accounts for relationship creativity to come to fruition in collaborative interdependence.

Writing in a 2002 *Harvard Business Review* article, Patrick Lencioni sees a "fad" that was created in the wake of the 1994 publication of *Built to Last* by Jim Collins and Jerry Porras. Collins and Porras observed that the best companies established and adhered to a set of core values. "Today, 80% of the *Fortune* 100 tout their values publicly—values that too often stand for nothing but a desire to be *au courant* or, worse still, politically correct."[85] Failing to give due process to identifying and communicating core values to employees can result in loss of leadership's credibility and poisonous cynicism among employees who can easily see when company leaders' actions do not correspond with stated values.

At the same time, Lencioni strongly affirms the vital importance of core values for companies that take the trouble to set values the right way. Core values create and sustain strong culture, helping the company be what it needs to be; strategically chosen aspirational values can lead the company toward healthy expansion and meaningful innovation. However, values need to be carefully selected, and the process must be given the time that is needed to reflect on what a value may mean in practice, in order to avoid pitfalls such as promoting a value that means one thing to the mindset that created it and another to corporate constituencies. For example, one company CEO postponed a values announcement long enough to discover that the value "transparent" meant something very different to the company's European employees than it did in the United States. The value was changed to "collaborative" to better express what leadership really intended.[86] Taking the time—and Lencioni emphases that this means months, not days—to put forward a set of values that will drive company cultures toward desired goals also means that core values be woven into everything employees do.

While core values are indeed important, Lencioni argues that any broadly collaborative approach to creating a set of core values is a bad idea. Surveying all employees to ask what they think the values should

---

85 Patrick M. Lencioni, "Make Your Values Mean Something," *Harvard Business Review (July, 2002)* 6.
86 Lencioni, 8.

be creates the impression that any input is acceptable, and invites participation even from employees that probably should not be in the company at all. "Values initiatives have nothing to do with building consensus—they're about imposing a set of fundamental, strategically strong beliefs on a broad group of people." Any employee who "can't embrace or embody these values" may belong at a different company.[87] Instead, he recommends carefully selecting a team of executives, company founders who may still be with the company, and key employees, and ensuring they take the time necessary to think through how the values they select might actually play out in the corridors.

We firmly agree that values must be carefully considered and their representative behaviors understood given the company's history, culture, business, and strategic aims. We also agree that any values initiative must be carefully undertaken and the potential risks involved must be evaluated. However, creating "strong beliefs" among a broad group of people is difficult at best if they do not see at least some of their own core values in operation. Imposing values on a work group or organization without consultation or acknowledgement of existing values expresses a Leader-As-Center leadership style (described in Part III above), corresponding to the aspects of the Family perspective which value authority and look to leadership to define the rules. Even if this style is familiar and even acceptable to employees, in some organizations, the psychology of reactance, originally described in the 1960s, is such that people react negatively to the perception of a loss of their freedom to choose. The magnitude of this reaction corresponds to the perceived magnitude of the loss, and the willingness to be persuaded is proportionally decreased. The reaction to forced imposition of values on group members or employees can indeed be poisonous.

A prudent approach to values alignment in organizations includes processes that provide for the buy-in of the organization's values by its members. People need to be able to look at the organizational values and say, to some degree or another, "I support that." As we have shown, there is a tremendously wide array of possible values that may result in people choosing effective behaviors aimed at a specific objective or mission. Getting the buy-in for group or organizational values is more important than the values themselves. It cannot be ignored that values are already in operation. Using an instrument such as the Values Perspectives survey can provide a picture of the values energy present in a company,

87 Ibid., 8.

i.e., identifies what values are actually in operation in the perception of employees. The energy already present can be used to identify key values that actually support the aims of the company. Because values cluster and key values are supported by other values, this identification can be crucial to understanding how employees, even in a large organization, can bring their own values energy to bear in supporting a company's stated values.

Whether or not an organization is surveyed, dialogue still has to occur, between leaders and employees, in groups, between managers and between manager and employee. Buy-in is achieved only through presenting a values set and having employees work through how they will live those values—and what expectations they may have of what it looks like for leadership to live them in ways that are recognizable to the company at large. Values in operation look very different at different organizational levels and in different functions. The value of responsibility looks very different behaviorally in the office than it does on a construction site.

Dialogue aimed at achieving basic agreements on what a value is, and is not, makes it possible for people to commit to it. As is always the case, new values can be chosen. Understanding the values substrate on which a company's culture already exists is necessary to taking the steps toward values shift. Values shift may be driven by the strategic aims of leadership with legitimate authority, but its success rests on the informed consent, commitment and behavioral alignment of the constituency.

An Example of Values Alignment

We received an emergency call. It seems that a consultant had attempted a values assessment intervention with a major group in a large not-for-profit organization. The disaster occurred when the results were presented with an unfortunate lack of preparation. The participants felt they were being told what to believe in, rather than what they had revealed through the survey they were given. This caused a near riot in the group, and soured the entire 70 person organization. With good reason, the CEO and senior team were worried about the negative impact on the organization's work.

This particular situation precluded the use of any sort of a survey, so we simply asked the VP of Human Resources to send an email to everyone asking for each person's 6 most important values as applied to his or her organizational work, in rank order. After tabulating the responses, we walked into a room with 70 suspicious and some still angry people. One look at the CEO's face said, "This had better work." She was, to put it mildly, anxious. Our agenda was simple; to get people engaged, and then by group consensus, decide on 5 or 6 values and their definitions. We had two sessions over two consecutive days. The first day was spent with a little explanation about the nature of values and what we were doing and a lot of time with people talking with partners, in small groups, and as a large group. At the end of the day people seemed okay, somewhat pleased, or at least curious. The CEO's expression was a little more relaxed, but she didn't stick around (not usually a good sign). She didn't realize all that group work was necessary trust building time so they could be genuine with each other the next day.

The second day we walked into a lot of group energy, somewhat skeptical, but still engaged. We immediately realized we had far too much planned for the time and had to break the first rule of consulting, "Deliver What You Have Prepared." So, we just went for the heart of the need and announced, "We need six values and definitions. We need everyone's input. This is a consensus decision. Will you participate in accordance with our ground rules (Respect, Listening, etc.)?" The answer was yes. So we facilitated a 70 person dialogue and got to 5 values and had crafted definitions that were customized for that specific environment. It seemed we were finished (we were exhausted). But when we asked the group if there was anything else, many people shouted, "Yes, we need one more." A quiet sigh (on our part), and then we were back at it. We finished with a standing ovation from the entire group, for the entire group. It was hard work, and people remarked that they had heard employees contribute whom they had not heard participate in any large meeting for 25 years.

The members of the organization had aligned along their own values. They had taken the time to discuss and craft the language, respectfully disagree and compromise, and eventually come to consensus on each value and definition. We did not have time to decide on representative behaviors. That was left for smaller groups as part of the assignment for the near future. The other part of the assignment was to revisit the original work in about a year and revise as necessary. Values are dynamic and their priority needs to be periodically revisited.

Using the Values Perspective Survey

The Values Perspective Survey is one of the most useful assessments we have in our toolkit. It is quite possible to do effective, successful values work without using any survey. That approach takes longer, and usually requires a lot more energy from both the coach or consultant and the participants. Often, the time required to participate in values discovery with a coach, or in values identification in a group, is time well-spent because of its developmental value. Pragmatically, most of the time we need to help people get to the point where they can begin as quickly as possible to validate their value selections, select additional values if desired, and establish value definitions—then identify behavioral options and move toward the process of testing behavioral options. The most immediate advantage of the survey is that it provides a relatively quick and efficient way of helping people identify their priorities and worldview. The survey is structured as follows:

1) The Individual Survey and Report. Surveying values always begins with the individual, as indeed values work should in general. An individual is presented with an internet-based survey structured such that the individual may compare values, select which is "more important" and which is "less important." In this way, an initial prioritization is achieved, from which the individual is guided through the selection of highest-priority values, in priority order. A simple algorithm calculates the values selections to determine the values perspective with the greatest concentration of values energy.

This selection process is a discernment exercise, and people taking the survey often report that it made them think about their values in a new way. An individual, confidential report that no one else ever sees except at the individual's behest is delivered electronically to the person when the survey is completed. The report includes a description of the perspective that has been identified through the individual's value choices, and explains how a perspective view characterizes the individual's likely worldview. No survey can measure with certainty what a person's perspective is in reality. This is ultimately a matter of discernment on the part of the individual. He or she will likely recognize aspects of his or her worldview in the perspective description. If not, he or she may recognize that another perspective better describes his or her general outlook. His or her chosen nine values are shown in priority-order. A list of discernment questions allows the individual to consider each value in light of their own experience, and to consider developmental options unique to each value. These questions are robust and are constructed using researched developmental models and practical pedagogy based on decades of coaching practice.[88]

For many individuals, the intervention may end here. Having gone through a discernment process and being provided with developmental

88 A sample of the individual Values Perspective survey report can be found at http://www.kairios.com.

questions for consideration, there is ample information for a person to continue on his or her values discernment process on his or her own.

2) A Tool for the Coach: The Coach's Field Report. When an individual takes The Values Perspective survey online, a further report may be generated from the database. This report shows all values in the Values Perspective field, arranged by perspective. The individual's core perspective and top nine highest-priority values are shown. In addition, all values selected during the survey process are shown. Similarly to a histogram, the values energy in each perspective, resulting from the individual's choice of values, is graphically represented. Using this report, a coach can initiate a discussion with a coachee that takes into account the deeper levels of values dynamics, such as reach, and Foundation, Focus and Vision value clusters. Because of its structure, possible values gaps are easy to graphically identify. This report also allows for formulating and testing potential values 'tracks' or other significant clusters that may enter the coaching discussion based on the coachee's intention or goals.

This report is provided to coaches in an individual coaching situation, who are certified in the use of the Values Perspective theory and model, and have demonstrated basic coaching skills. The most important skills are 1) the ability to provide a safe environment, free from judgment or bias; 2) the ability to formulate testable hypotheses using the data at hand, and within the context of the coachee's situation and the coaching brief; and 3) the ability to formulate and ask appropriate questions that help the coachee to arrive at clarity.

3) A Tool for the Facilitator and/or Consultant: The Aggregated Field Report. Individual survey data may be grouped to construct an aggregated report. It is similar to the Coach's Field Report, except that it anonymously displays an averaging of all values choices made by a group of individuals. As with the Coach's Report, a graphic representation of the values field provides, in effect, a histogram/snapshot of the group's values energy, and is a powerful focus for stimulating objective discussion and dialogue within a group, starting from the safe foundation of anonymity. Once a facilitator or consultant communicates the basic factors needed to understand how values work, participants in a group setting can quickly see:

- likely sources for communication successes and misfires, within the group and with other functional groups, partners or customers;
- perspective gaps (for example, groups will often conclude that they would like to focus more values energy in the Relational perspective);
- values diversity within the group.

When these observations begin to surface and group dialogue is stimulated, the survey and reports have done their work and can be put aside for the time being.

Diversity in a group is an extremely important issue. The Values Perspective Survey results, when showing an aggregate of a working group's values selections, immediately changes the concept of diversity from one that is defined by gender, age, ethnicity, or other demographic, to one that is defined by perspective and values energy that is potentially available to the group as a whole through its diversity. People who might otherwise be thought of as "outliers" may be re-defined as essential resources that contribute something important for the success of the group. Not that gender, age, and ethnicity are not important, they can be, and should be considered and discussed when they are problematic. But values differences will always be present, and that is a good thing. Once a group understands this, then sensitive diversity topics can be discussed more respectfully, and more successfully. The Values Perspective model and survey make a strong case *for* diversity.

Finally, survey results quickly show two things: that energy can be redirected, and where that redirected energy might be aimed. Using the survey as a tool, both individuals and groups often very quickly identify what needs to be prioritized or re-prioritized in order to achieve stated objectives.

Consulting with the Aggregated Field Report

The Aggregated Field Report can be useful to consultants, since it permits the collection of values data across groups for comparison and contrast, for example, between selected functional groups within an organization. A caveat for this kind of use is that any organizational intervention will cause its own, sometimes unintended consequences, and organizational leadership is always responsible to ensure ethical use of survey results and to anticipate questions or challenges that may arise among their constituents, and their appropriate resolution.

This report can be very useful in internal or external marketing. For example, the survey was administered over a 4-year period to successive student cohorts in the capstone course of a specialized MBA program, creating a database of several hundred participants. The data showed that, for the most part, year after year, people with extremely similar values sets were self-selecting into the program, which provided a highly targeted values-based marketing platform for the degree program. The data also showed a consistent and glaring gap between the students' aggregate values perspective in comparison to the general values perspective profile of for-profit corporations. This yielded two benefits. First, the educators were able to use the data to show how the program curriculum should be adjusted to give greatest benefit to the graduates. Second, the data were shared with the students as part of the capstone course, which occurred as they were about to enter or re-enter the workforce. With this information, in a few hours, the students were able to come up with ways to bridge that gap, formulating communication and influence strategies. Their understanding of values perspectives provided insights they could use to enhance their credibility and provide more effective opportunities for mutual understanding between themselves and prospective employers, partners or investors.

Final Words

It would not be appropriate to head this section as "Conclusion" because now you know too much about values and how they work not to be engaged in, at least your own process of making yourself more effective, communicating more authentically, and understanding more accurately. However, we have a saying, "Just because you know about something, does not mean you can do it." This applies to nearly everything, but it is particularly appropriate to working with values. Understanding more about values may lead us to believe we have mastered the process. It seems that a false sense of control occurs when we become intellectually familiar with a subject, allowing us to feel like we have incorporated it into behavior and thinking.

We may go to seminars and take courses, and we quickly admit and understand that successful completion of courses does not guarantee complete understanding of the subject. Working with values presents us with opportunities to examine ourselves at a level not usually available. We are confronted with the challenge of first deciding what we like about ourselves, and why, and then deciding how we might want to make changes, however slight, to improve who we are, and what we can be. A common error is to forget the difference between the abstract description, like a survey report, and what it represents. "The map is not the territory" is a statement that should be regularly revisited when doing this work, to keep us grounded on who we are in the here and now, and not only focused on who we want to become. [89]

89 S. I . Hayakawa, *Language in Thought and Action*, (New York: Harcourt, Brace and World, 1964).

We have written this book with several groups of people in mind. First are those that are interested in their own, personal development, and are exploring values as a means to that process. To you we say, "Congratulations. You have chosen to do the deep work, to go into the genuine aspects of who you are, how you make sense of the world, and how you relate to it, and everyone in it." This is good work. It will lead you to deeper realms of understanding, and eventually a satisfying ability to respond to two of the most powerful questions we have encountered; questions we have previously referred to that are posed by Michael L. Ray, but that may now have more significance for you, "Who is my Self?" and "What is my Work?" Much of the continuing journey ahead of you will take the form of metaphor, but when it does, you can always probe those metaphors to reveal their underlying values and the priorities they suggest. This will serve you well.

Also, we have had in mind practitioners. Managers, executives, coaches, and consultants that do, or would like to do, values work with others. It is our hope you will have found useful insights regarding values, the dynamics of values, and how to work with them in ways which will serve those with whom you work. This is not simple, "one-off" work. It requires both commitment and courage. It requires that you, as that practitioner, be able to create and hold a safe space so that people can reveal and discuss those things that are truly most dear to them, their values. This, once it has been established, is what we call sacred space. It is our extreme hope that you will both respect that space and hold it well, because we well know that when you do, and when you can also "get out of the way," that is manage your own presence in that space, wonderful things happen for individuals and groups. Things for which you can only take partial credit. Nevertheless, it is good work, when you can get it.

We tell potential organizational clients that this work does take time and energy, and moreover, is potentially hazardous. Organizational life often takes a great toll on people, and this sort of work gives them a perfect opportunity to release pent up energy that they may have been holding within for many years. If they are looking for a quick fix to an organizational problem, this is not the path for them. So to you the practitioner, we say, when you do values work, the release of some of that energy is a real potential. Tread carefully, respectfully; you will be exceedingly successful.

Values are dynamic and changeable. For this reason alone, no two people or situations present the same values profile. There is always more to learn.

Frequently Asked Values Questions (FAVQs)

How are values different from beliefs?

A belief is a conviction or confidence in something that we hold to be true or accept without having a full knowledge or understanding. Beliefs may change as a result of strongly transformative life experiences, but will tend to persist as a foundational aspect of our personality. A value is different, in that it is a concept that operates to prioritize importance for us, and guides decision making and behavioral choices. Not all values are continually held within waking, daily consciousness, but to the degree values are conscious—and this usually includes the cluster we refer to as Focus values, which drive daily thoughts and choices—they can be changed or re-prioritized. Some observers make the distinction between beliefs, attitudes and values, such that attitudes arise from core beliefs and in turn characterize value choices. Others may explain the difference as a matter of believing and thinking, in other words, while beliefs may be inviolate, how we think and thus, act is changeable.

Can values change? How?

True story: The first time one of us received values coaching, the coach diplomatically pointed out that no values had been selected in a particular perspective. Given the situational responsibilities at the time, it was obvious that there was going to be a need to draw on values and associated skills that had been previously ignored. Reports are not always good news, and this one created a feeling of imminent failure. So the question to him was "What should I do?"

He smiled, and kindly said, "Why don't you pick a couple you think you are going to need to draw on in the future."

The response was immediate, and revealed some lack of understanding about values, "You mean I can just *choose* them?"

"Why not?" He replied. "They're *your* values."

Selecting new values is relatively easy. Developing skills to support those new values can be much more difficult. But once the awareness and need is established, one is much more motivated to do so. It may take a while, and it is possible the behavioral choices that emerge from re-prioritizing values may never feel like one's greatest strengths. However, valuing these concepts results in the conscious capacity to direct energy toward operationalizing them.

The purpose of creating a values profile for a person or a group is to provide the opportunity to consider, discuss, and change if change is thought to be needed. Ideally, a profile would have some values operating in every perspective. In actual life, we all have a perspective we use the most, which is our core perspective. It is possible to over-emphasize that perspective. If so, that invites the opportunity to change. We all also have a perspective that receives the least attention and energy, and may require more attention than we currently give it. This also invites the question of the need to change.

How many values are there?

A very large number, when we consider the technical answer to the question. No one really knows, but potentially thousands of concepts that are sufficiently linguistically precise that might be thought of and used as values for a person or group. But practically speaking, the answer depends on what you want to find out. We have used enough for a person or group to be able to make an informed selection from each perspective. While there does not seem to be a set, minimum number to present a sufficiently large list to allow for survey-takers to make meaningful differentiations, it is our experience that number is somewhere around one hundred. Values tend to be more numerous in the typical focus clusters. So, it is reasonable to include in any survey more values from those perspectives than others.

Can values actually be measured?

Not exactly. Values themselves, as has been suggested in the characteristics above, are intangible, and held by each of us internally, so they cannot be directly measured. There are a variety of surveys and assessments that attempt to identify what one's values actually are.

Values assessments measure one's choices regarding values. Therefore, when using any sort of survey or assessment, each person receiving a report of some sort must ask and answer the question, "Is this really me? Do these values really describe what is important to me?" We call that a "self-validation process," and consider it to be essential. If the answer is "Yes, these are my values," then one may continue with refining that those values mean, and how they operate. If the answer is "No," we suggest a person refer to an overall list of values and consider what is missing from his or her own list.

Values are tricky, and attempting to measure them is like trying to hit a moving target. The reason is not so much that values are dynamic, which they are, but it is much more the case that each of us is constantly moving from one situation to another, which changes our perception of how a given value operates, and the priority in which we place it. Values need to be pinned down in terms of definition and structure well enough for us to be able to work with them, but not so much that our descriptions of them destroy the very energy they represent.

The societal-level values measures discussed in Part II of this book are robust because they measure values—at country levels, not individually—through sets of values questions associated with context descriptors and observations and may even take into account "soft" evidence such as the character of public monuments. Their value is in periodic repetition, giving rise to data that can be interpreted through differing theoretical lenses that propose explanations for shifts in values. Nevertheless, individual values can differ greatly from societal norms.

Are Values Predictive?

Values are highly ambiguous, so even after discussions between parties on what their shared values should be, even after careful agreed upon definitions, and supporting behavioral examples, new or undiscovered interpretations of a given value are not only quite possible, depending on shifting situations, but are quite likely. So at a group level, with careful assessment, we might make a prediction analogous to weather predictions, which are made in terms of probability. That is, if a group agrees on a set of values, we might predict that over time, we would *probably* be able to observe supporting behaviors. But at an individual level, such a prediction would be somewhat foolhardy because of the complex and dynamic nature of both the individual psyche and the situational contexts in which he or she operates.

However, on a personal level, we make predictions all the time regarding our friends, family, people we work with as well as people we do not even know. Humans are habitual, and behave in patterned ways, so if we are familiar with someone, or extrapolate from a set of behaviors we have witnessed, we stand a pretty good chance of making a prediction with some confidence of being correct. When we are correct in our guesses, we congratulate ourselves on being a "good judge of character." When we are wrong, we usually attribute that misdirected prediction to an external influence that is or was beyond our control.

Neither people's behavior nor values are so complicated that we are without the means to understand them. You can take some comfort in the fact that our perception and understanding is determined by our general core perspective and worldview, and this does not tend to change with changing situations. So even though values may change locations on our individual priority list, the way we understand both our values and the situations that may cause temporary shifting to occur depends on that overall perspective.

Is There a Difference Between Individual Values and Group Values?

This distinction is one of the first significant conceptual questions regarding values that surfaced in philosophical writings, an individual orientation being concerned with individual motivation and development, and a group or collective orientation concerning the impact of values on a group as a whole and tending to emphasize the institutional or cultural origins of values. In many models, the continuum of values is explicitly identified in terms of the degree to which an individual is subject to conventional imposition of values, suggesting a greater degree of moral development when one is "free" from such convention. It is useful to recognize individual/group distinction or focus and the influence the two concepts have on our views on values and systems of ethics; these issues are important for both coaches and consultants to explore with clients. It is not surprising that many theorists have built these concepts into their respective models. However, while we have found that an understanding of values in these terms is useful, building them into a model is far too restrictive to be useful. That is, values are much more ambiguous and dynamic than a binary individual/group categorization suggests. We have avoided this distinction in terms of either perspective or single-value identifications for several reasons.

- First, a strict Individual vs. Group categorization simply cannot be defended. There are many examples where a single value can be held by both, with different resulting behaviors.
- Second, the structure of the values continuum does not logically suggest this designation, so it appears to us it has been imposed on the larger pool of values to help manage them, but this is a forced imposition.
- Third, we are operating with our own guiding principle of simplifying the presentation of values theory as much as possible, so as to provide people with effective tools. In our view, all values measurement should lead toward dialogue that takes into account context and transparently states basic goals and intentions.

What is the Difference Between Terminal or Ends and Instrumental or Means Values?

Some authors (Rokeach, Hall, and Beck and Cowan among them) make a structural distinction between two types of values, using such terms as "terminal and instrumental," "goals and means," or "what" and "how." Making this distinction can be problematic because values are dynamic, and can change functions easily. Values do function as goals or the desired end state of some process, *and* as means or the process by which those ends are achieved. But a single value can change from operating as a goal to a way to achieve other goals, and thus, become the means to the next goal. A high school diploma or college degree representing the value of Education is a good example of this change in function from goal to means. Before graduation, it is a goal, after graduation it becomes the means to securing a job that requires such a diploma. It can also refer to further use of what one has learned in the job, or perhaps simply knowing how to continue to learn. Because of this ability to change function, it is not possible to insist that a value functions in only one way, or to be able to predict when it will change function from operating as a goal to operating as a means to another goal. Additionally, cultural influences involving gender and age (generation) can also influence the goals/means designation.

By not designating values in this way, we allow each person to interpret how a particular value operates, and if it changes function for that person, that does not necessarily change his or her overall perspective. Nor does the shift from goal to means (or the reverse) change the perspective in which a given value is usually found. However, it has been our experience that, when values are concerned, we must avoid suggesting too rigid or structured a model to allow for each person and group to designate and define, by example, how a given value is functioning in this regard. This same point is argued by Stanley Riukas, who suggests that values are reversible in terms of these two functions, and implies that the designation is a functional one, that describes a characteristic of values in general.[90]

Are there bad values?

This is one of the biggest perennial value questions. Aren't greed, violence, hate, dishonesty, manipulation and coercion values too? Our work is oriented toward helping individuals and groups to develop themselves and improve their relationships, and with that general orientation in mind, we have decided not to include so called negative values in the Values Perspective theory, model, and survey. However, we must acknowledge that given our definition of a value as *a human quality, arranged or structured by relative priority, or importance, and manifested through language and behavior*, any number of negative values might operate in a person's life, or in a group culture. We do not pretend that negative values do not operate as priorities in all of us, at one time or another. We all have a shadow side to us. Suffice it to say that just like positive values, there are a great number of negative ones. We are sure you are aware of them, and perhaps far too familiar with some of them.

So it is useful to point out two conditions whereby values, even what we think of as generally positive values, can be used to the detriment of others. The first is manipulation, which is a type of interpersonal

90 Stanley Riukas, "Inherent and Instrumental Values in Ethics" (paper presented at the Twentieth World Congress of Philosophy, Boston, Massachusetts, August 10-15, 1998), accessed July 12, 2013 http://www.bu.edu/wcp/Papers/Valu/ValuRiuk.htm.

power, but is by definition unethical. Manipulation occurs when critical or necessary information is distorted or withheld so that others cannot come to accurate understanding of an issue, and subsequently cannot make informed decisions about that issue, or will be directed to make decisions which run counter to what would have been decided if an accurate or complete understanding were available. A hidden agenda is one example of manipulation. By definition, a hidden agenda is an objective unknown to the person(s) being influenced. A hidden agenda is often veiled in ambiguous language, and often makes use of selective statistical data so as to give the illusion of fact. It is an inversion of the value of Informing, which is to provide information. In this case, the information is intended to mislead.

We have previously discussed ethics and the role values play in the operation of ethics. It is not difficult to understand how having knowledge of the value priorities of another person or group of people allows for the deliberate triggering of energy and subsequent behavioral motivation toward an objective which that person or that group would not otherwise intend. Nevertheless, on any given day, we can find examples in politics or commercial advertising where values are being triggered in ethically questionable ways.

In our work, we have observed that incorporating coerced or negative values tends to fall into patterns which are similar to the patterns by which positive values are incorporated, because the characteristics of values discussed earlier apply to all values. One pattern, in particular, may be useful to point out because it helps explain how a value can be either positive or negative in its effect. This brings us to the second condition by which values can be used negatively.

We will use Respect as an example. Generally, respect is a value that is foundational to all sustainable human relationships. Without it, we simply won't tolerate a relationship unless there are extreme, extenuating circumstances associated with a particular situation. When it is present, an individual acts as the owner of the value and shows his or her respect in a variety of ways to another person or group of people, and may reasonably hope to receive respect reciprocally in most circumstances. The individual is the subject, respect is the verb, or a part of the predicate, and the person being respected is the object, the receiver of the respect. All well and good. But, it is possible for an individual to turn that structure around, and while prioritizing respect, places him- or herself in the position of being the object. In that case, respect is imposed on or demanded of the other while being prioritized by the individual.

This inversion can occur with any number of values and you can easily imagine what it looks like when values such as Self Worth, Financial Success, Achievement, Listening, or Trust are used in this way. When this inversion does occur, we call it evil because it fundamentally violates the integrity of the other person. We concede that the concept of evil is larger than this example, but we believe that when it does occur, and we have seen it in action more than once, its effects are negative and harmful.

There is a moral aspect to working with values, and while we refrain from including values in the Values Perspective survey that are negative at face value so as to limit any hint of a priori judgment, nevertheless, in terms of the application of one's values, questions of morality and ethics, or in extreme cases, pathology, are unavoidable. Morally, too, some instances of what we may consider "evil" may lead to conundrums when we attribute unqualifiedly negative meanings to intents or actions without full knowledge of context. We could easily be wrong. That is why, when we survey values, we do so in order for a dialogue to occur, whether it be internal, with a coach or counselor, with peers, or in a carefully facilitated large group context.

Sources for The Values Perspective

When constructing the list of 102 values used in this current work, we consulted a number of sources to ensure the current list was well founded. For example, if a value or need showed up in several sources, we wanted to include it. At the same time, we have made sure, by refining the definitions that anyone reading them, regardless of their orientation or situation, would be able to identify and relate to them. This avoids some of the problems that previous writers have encountered when writing from a particular context. The same reasoning was employed to identify which stage a specific value would be located.

Directly consulted resources for stage and value identifications include:

- Abraham Maslow: Comparison to stages and to "B-values" (Being values are those that drive personal development and are considered to be positive), and to "D-values" (Deficient values are those that act to motivate as unfulfilled needs, and do not drive development). [Abraham Maslow, Henry Geiger, and Bertha G. Maslow, *The Farther Reaches of Human Nature* (New York: Penguin Books, 1971).]

- Milton Rokeach: Consideration of Terminal and Instrumental values with the Goals and Means of Brian Hall's model. [Milton Rokeach, *Understanding Human Values* (New York: The Free Press, 1973).]

- Lawrence Kohlberg: The identification of stages as markers of both life stages and moral development as they compare to Perspectives in the current model. [Lawrence Kohlberg, *The Psychology of Moral Development: The Nature and Validity of Moral Stages* (San Francisco: Harper and Row, 1984).]

- Robert Freed Bales: His SYMLOG group assessment instrument is values based and explicitly tied to behavior. Consideration of the values identified in the SYMLOG Value Statement Rating Form. [Robert Freed Bales and Stephen P. Cohen, *Symlog, A System for the Multiple Level Observation of Groups* (New York: Free Press, 1979), 503-504.]

- Brian Hall: His book, not widely available, called *Values Shift,* identifies 125 values, about half of which are compound values. [Brian P. Hall, *Values Shift* (Rockport, MA: Twin Lights Publishers, Inc., 1995), 225-235.]

- Both Scott Bristol and Paul Chippendale have developed "second generation" models that originally drew heavily on Hall's work, but then have revised and refined their own work. [Scott Bristol: LJMap, 2007, http://www.ljmap.com/; and Clare Colins and Paul Chippendale, *New Wisdom II: Values Based Development* (Brisbane, Australia: Acorn Publications, 1995).]

- The recent work published by the Gallup organization has identified values in the form of individual strengths and group characteristics. [We consulted two sources in particular, Marcus Buckingham and Donald O. Clifton, Now, *Discover Your Strengths* (New York: The Free Press, 2001), 81-116; and Marcus Buckingham and Curt Coffman, *First Break All The Rules* (New York: Simon and Schuster, 1999), 250-267.]

- KAI: The Kirton Adaption Innovation Inventory, developed by Michael Kirton, is a self-assessment instrument that identifies different styles of problem solving and creativity, particularly in terms of idea generation, efficiency, and the influence of convention and conformity. [Michael Kirton, Ed., *Adaptors and Innovators* (London: Routledge, 1989).]

- MBTI: The Myers-Briggs Type Indicator is the most widely used self-assessment instrument available. It identifies cognitive styles and preferred ways of interaction, information perception and organization, decision-making, and structure. [Isabel Briggs-Myers, *Introduction to Type*, 6th ed. (Palo Alto, CA: Consulting Psychologists Press, Inc. 1998).]

- The Fundamental Interpersonal Relations Orientation — Behavior instrument (FIRO-B) was originally developed by William Schutz, and is now owned and administered by Consulting Psychologists Press. The concept of relationship, particularly in terms of its component driving forces is useful both in terms of specific values, and to the descriptions of several stages. [William C. Schutz, *FIRO: A Three Dimensional Theory of Interpersonal Behavior* (New York: Holt, Rinehart, & Winston, 1958).]

- The GLOBE study led by Robert House, shows both particular values and indicates perspective like orientations for those values, which are found worldwide, particularly in regard to leadership. [*Culture, Leadership, and Organizations: The GLOBE Study of 62 Societies*. Robert J. House, Paul J. Hanges, Mansour Javidan, Peter W. Dorfman, and Vipin Gupta, eds. (Thousand Oaks, CA: Sage Publications, 2004).]

- All of the contributions surveyed above had had an influence on the current work. Many times the salient points made by different authors were either redundant or at least had a direct relationship to our major sources. These are secondary sources, and we have consulted them all, to various degrees.

- Personal conversations with, and questions from, scholars, coaches, consultants, and clients over the past 20+ years, in both Europe and the U.S.

REFERENCES

About Learning, "What is 4MAT?" Accessed December 12, 2013. http://www.aboutlearning.com/what-is-4mat.

Amabile, Teresa M. and Stanley Gryskiewicz. *Creativity in the R&D Laboratory*. Technical Report No. 30, Center for Creative Leadership, 1987.

Amabile, Teresa M. *Creativity in Context*. Boulder, CO: Westview Press, 1996.

Bales, Robert Freed and Stephen P. Cohen. *Symlog, A System for the Multiple Level Observation of Groups*. New York: Free Press, 1979.

Barrett, Richard. *Building a Values-Driven Organization*. Burlingame, MA: Butterworth-Heinemann, 2006.

Beck, Don Edward and Christoper C. Cowan. *Spiral Dynamics: Mastering Values, Leadership, and Change*. Malden, MA: Blackwell Publishing, 1996.

Block, Peter. *Stewardship*. San Francisco: Barrett-Koehler Publishers, 1996.

Brehm, Jack. W. *A Theory of Psychological Reactance*. New York: Academic Press, 1966.

Briggs-Myers, Isabel. *Introduction to Type,* 6th Ed. Palo Alto, CA: Consulting Psychologists Press, Inc., 1998.

Briggs-Myers, Isabel, Mary H. McCaulley, Naomi L. Quenk and Allen L. Hammer. *MBTI Manual: A Guide to the Development and Use of the Myers Briggs Type Indicator*, 3rd Ed. Palo Alto, CA: Consulting Psychologists Press, Inc. 1989.

Bristol, Scott. LJMap, 2007. Accessed July 16, 2013. http://www.ljmap.com/.

Buckingham, Marcus and Donald O. Clifton. *Now, Discover Your Strengths*. New York: The Free Press, 2001.

Buckingham, Marcus and Curt Coffman. *First Break All the Rules.* New York: Simon and Schuster, 1999.

Colins, Claire and Paul Chippendale. *New Wisdom II: Values Based Development*. Brisbane, Australia: Acorn Publications, 1995.

Crain, William C. *Theories of Development*. Upper Saddle River, NJ: Prentice Hall, 1985.

Damasio, Antonio. *The Feeling of What Happens: Body, Emotion and the Making of Consciousness*. London: Heinemann, 2004.

Daniels, Tom. D. and Barry K. Spiker. *Perspectives on Organizational Communication, 3rd. Ed.* Madison, WI: Brown & Benchmark Publishers, 1994.

De Ciantis, Cheryl and Kenton Hyatt. *Looking for Work with Values*, 2009. Accessed July 2, 2013. http://www.kairios.com.

Deetz, Stanley A., Sarah J. Tracy and Jennifer Lyn Simpson. *Leading Organizations through Transitions: Communication and Cultural Change*. Thousand Oaks, CA: Sage, 2000.

Denison, Daniel. R. *Corporate Culture and Organizational Effectiveness*. New York: John Wiley & Sons, 1990.

Erikson, Erik. *Childhood and Society*. New York: Norton, 1950.

Fowler, James. *Stages of Faith*. San Francisco: Harper and Row, 1971.

Goleman, Daniel. *Emotional Intelligence*. New York: Bantam Books, 1995.

Greenleaf, Robert K. *Servant Leadership*. Mahwah, NJ: Paulist Press, 1991.

Hall, Brian. P. *Values Shift*. Rockport, MA: Twin Lights Publishers, Inc., 1995.

Hampton-Turner, Charles. *Charting the Corporate Mind*. New York: The Free Press, 1990.

Hayakawa, S. I. *Language in Thought and Action*. New York: Harcourt, Brace and World, 1964.

Hofstede, Geert, and Michael H. Bond "Hofstede's Culture Dimensions: An Independent Validation Using Rokeach's Value Survey." *Journal of Cross-Cultural-Psychology* 15 (December 1988), 417-433.

Hofstede, Geert. *Cultures Consequences: Comparing Values, Behaviors, Institutions and Organizations Across Nations*. Beverly Hills, CA: Sage, 2001.

Hoppe, Michael. H. "Culture and Leader Effectiveness: The GLOBE Study" (9/18/2007). Accessed July 3, 2013. http://www.inspireimagineinnovate.com/PDF/GLOBEsummary-by-Michael-H-Hoppe.pdf.

House, Robert J., Paul J. Hanges, Mansour Javidian, Peter W. Dorfman, and Vipin Gupta, eds. *Culture, Leadership, and Organizations: The GLOBE Study of 62 Societies*. Thousand Oaks, CA: Sage Publications, 2004.

Hyatt, Kenton and Cheryl De Ciantis. "Values Driven Leadership." *Integral Leadership Review*, October, 2012. Accessed August 12, 2013. http://integralleadershipreview.com/7601-values-driven-leadership/.

Infante, Dominic, Theodore Avtgis, and Andrew Rancer, *Contemporary Communication Theory.* Dubuque, IA: Kendall Hunt, 2010.

Inglehart, Ronald and Christian Welzel. "Changing Mass Priorities: The Link Between Modernization and Democracy." *Perspectives on Politics*, 121, no. 2 (June 2010), 551-567. Accessed January 15, 2014. http://www.worldvaluessurvey.org/wvs/articles/folder_published/publication_587/files/ChangingMassPriorities.pdf.

Kant, Immanuel. *Groundwork of the Metaphysics of Morals.* Translated by Mary J. Gregor and Jens Timmerman. New York: Cambridge University Press, 1998.

Keenan, Thomas and Subhadra Evans. *An Introduction to Child Development*, 2d ed. Thousand Oaks, CA: Sage, 2009.

Kirton. Michael J., Ed. *Adaptors and Innovators: Styles of Creativity and Problem Solving*. London: Routledge, 1989.

Kohlberg, Lawrence. *The Psychology of Moral Development: The Nature and Validity of Moral Stages*. San Francisco: Harper and Row, 1984.

Kuhn, Thomas. *The Structure of Scientific Revolutions*. Chicago: University of Chicago Press, 1962.

Kurtzke, Christian. "Barriers and Enablers to Business Transformation towards the Knowledge Economy." Paper presented at the European Foundation for Management Development Special Event "Does Learning Pay?" Chipping Norton, England, September 27-29, 1998.

Lencioni, Patrick M. "Make Your Values Mean Something." *Harvard Business Review*, July 2002.

Leslie, Jean Brittain and Phillip Braddy. *Benchmarks*. Greensboro, NC: Center for Creative Leadership, 2013. Accessed October 10, 2013. http://www.ccl.org/leadership/pdf/assessments/BenchmarksTechnicalManual.pdf.

Lombardo, Michael, Robert W. Eichinger, and Roger P. Pearman. *You: Being More Effective in Your MBTI Type*. Minneapolis, MN: Lominger International, Inc., 2005.

Maslow, Abraham. H. *Motivation and Personality,* 2d ed. New York: Harper and Row, 1970.

Maslow, Abraham, Henry Geiger, and Bertha G. Maslow. *The Farther Reaches of Human Nature.* New York: Penguin Books, 1971.

McCarthy, Bernice and Clif St. Germain. *The 4MAT Research Guide: Reviews of Literature on Individual Differences and Hemispheric Specialization and their Influence on Learning*. Barrington, IL: Excel, Inc., 1996.

McClelland, David. *The Achieving Society*. Princeton, NJ: Van Nostrand, 1961.

McLeod, Saul. "Jean Piaget: Cognitive Theory." Simply Psychology, 2009, updated 2012. Accessed July 8, 2012. http://www.simplypsychology.org/piaget.html.

Mealiea, Laird, and Ramon Baltazar. "A Strategic Guide for Building Effective Teams." *Public Personnel Management,* 34, no. 2 (Summer, 2005). Accessed September 15, 2103. http://www.questia.com/PM.qst?a=o&d=5012090317.

Mill, John Stuart. *Utilitarianism*, ed. George Sher. Indianapolis, IN: Hackett Publishing Inc., 2001.

Murray, Henry. A. *Explorations in Personality.* New York: Oxford University Press, 1938.

Nussbaum, Martha. *The Fragility of Goodness*. New York: Cambridge University Press, 1986.

NVC Consulting, “Spiral Dynamics FAQ Caveats and Concerns.” Accessed January 20, 2014. http://spiraldynamics.org/faq-caveats-and-concerns/.

Piaget, Jean. *The Psychology of the Child.* New York: Basic Books, 1972.

Plato. *Meno.* Translated by Benjamin Jowett. Whitefish, MT: Kessinger Publishing, 2004.

Plato. *Laches or Courage*. Translated by Benjamin Jowett. Accessed July 7, 2010. http://philosophy.eserver.org/plato/laches.txt.

Powell, James. *The Tao of Symbols*. New York: Quill, 1982.

Ray, Michael L. *Two Questions*. Unpublished manuscript, 2004.

Rest, James R., Darcia Narvaez, Stephen J. Thoma, and Muriel J. Bebeau. “A Neo-Kohlbergian Approach: The DIT and Schema Theory”. *Educational Psychology Review,* 11, no.4 (December, 1999). 291-324.

Riukas, Stanley. “Inherent and Instrumental Values in Ethics.” Paper presented at theTwentieth World Congress of Philosophy, Boston, Massachusetts, August 10-15, 1998. Accessed July 12, 2013. http://www.bu.edu/wcp/Papers/Valu/ValuRiuk.htm.

Rokeach, Milton. *Understanding Human Values.* New York: The Free Press, 1973.

Rotter, Julian B. “Generalized Expectancies for Internal Versus External Control of Reinforcement.” *Psychological Monographs: General and Applied 80*, no. 1 (1966) 1-28.

Scharmer, C. Otto. *Theory U: Leading from the Future as it Emerges*. Cambridge, MA: Society for Organizational Learning, Inc., 2007.

Schutz, William. C. FIRO: A *Three Dimensional Theory of Interpersonal Behavior*. New York: Holt, Rinehart, & Winston, 1958.

Schwartz, Shalom H. "A Theory of Cultural Values and Some Implications for Work." *Applied Psychology: An International Review* 48, no. 1 (January, 1999). 23-47.

Schwartz Value Survey. Accessed July 10, 2013. http://www.imo-international.de/index_englisch.htm?/englisch/html/svs_info_en.htm.

Shalom H. Schwartz. "An Overview of the Schwartz Theory of Basic Values." Online Readings in Psychology and Culture, 2(1), December 1, 2012. Accessed July 10, 2013. http://scholarworks.gvsu.edu/cgi/viewcontent.cgi?article=1116&context=orpc.

Singh, R. and Ho Yan Soo. "Attitudes and Attraction: A New Test of the Attraction, Repulsion and Similarity-Dissimilarity Asymmetry Hypotheses." *British Journal of Social Psychology* 39, no. 2 (June, 2000). 197-211.

Smith, Peter. B., and Shalom H. Schwartz. "Values." *Handbook of Cross-Cultural Psychology*, Vol. 3, 2d ed. Edited by John W. Berry, Marshall H. Segall and Cigdem Kagitçibasi. Boston: Allyn & Bacon, 1997. 77-118.

Triandis, Harry C. *Individualism & Collectivism*. Boulder, CO: Westview, 1995.

Turiel, Elliot. *The Culture of Morality: Social Development, Context, and Conflict* Cambridge, England: Cambridge University Press, 2002.

Wilson, Meena Surie, Ellen Van Velsor, Anand Chandrasekar and Corey Criswell. "Grooming Top Leaders: Cultural Perspectives from China, India, Singapore and the United States." White Paper. Center for Creative Leadership, 2013. Accessed November 2, 2013. http://www.ccl.org/leadership/pdf/research/GroomingTopLcadcrs.pdf.

World Values Survey. Accessed July 12, 2013. http://www.worldvaluessurvey.org/.

About the Authors

Kenton Hyatt, Ph.D., specializing in communication, values and creativity, is an international facilitator, trainer, executive coach and program designer. Kenton's particular areas of expertise include values assessment and development for individuals, teams and organizations; creativity assessment and development; and coaching managers to be coaches. Dr. Hyatt uses interactive learning methods based on psychological and behavioral assessment integrated with creative methodologies to produce active learning environments which are designed to achieve the results that are best suited for each person, group and organization. He is also an accomplished painter, photographer and storyteller. He holds certifications in a wide variety of individual, group, and organizational assessment instruments and programs. Kenton has taught communication at Rochester Institute of Technology and Humboldt State University. He was European Program Director for the Center for Creative Leadership; Director of Educational Programs at Values Technology; and Senior Trainer for Granite Construction. In 2001, Kenton and his wife and collaborative partner, Dr. Cheryl De Ciantis, founded their company, Kairios, and Kenton and Cheryl are the co-authors of the Values Perspective personal and group values survey. Dr. Hyatt has worked with executives and management groups from corporations including Bayer, Eastman Chemical, General Motors, Georgia Tech Institute for Leadership and Entrepreneurship, Granite Construction, Inc., Holy Innocents Episcopal School System, Miller Brewing, Motorola, Oracle, PepsiCo, Presidio School of Management, Procter and Gamble, Readers' Digest, Santa Clara Valley Medical Center, Schnitzer Steel, Teichert Construction and Aggregates, Unilever, United Way, Valent Biosciences U.S.A., Wallenius Wilhelmsen Lines, and Whirlpool Italy.

Cheryl De Ciantis, Ph.D. is an experienced international consultant, program and learning simulation designer, facilitator and executive coach. Since 1985, Cheryl has been associated with the Center for Creative Leadership and she served as Director of the Center's Brussels, Belgium campus. In 2001, Cheryl co-founded Kairios. Cheryl has designed and delivered programs, interventions and in-depth executive coaching in corporate, educational and not-for profit organizations that include Avery-Dennison, AT&T, Bayer, Georgia Tech Institute for Leadership and Entrepreneurship, Google, Granite Construction Inc., Habitat for Humanity, IBM, Ingersoll-Rand, Miller Brewing,

Motorola, Netherlands Organisation for Applied Scientific Research (TNO), North Carolina School for the Deaf, Oracle, PepsiCo Foods and Beverages International, PPG, Presidio Graduate School, Unilever Home and Personal Care Europe, Values Technology, Inc., Whirlpool Italy, and numerous others. Dr. De Ciantis is certified in the use of numerous psychological and cognitive instruments and 360° feedback surveys. A specialist in creativity and herself an artist, writer and storyteller, Cheryl obtained her doctorate in Mythological Studies with an emphasis in Depth Psychology from Pacifica Graduate Institute, which houses the Joseph Campbell Library, where she initiated her research into the intersection of art, technology and culture. A pioneer in creating and documenting creative/reflective learning methodologies in leadership development, Cheryl is the author of many articles and of *Using an Art Technique to Facilitate Leadership Development*.

More About Values Perspectives

For more information on Values Perspectives, including white papers and additional publications, visit kairios.com. We train OD specialists, talent managers, external and internal consultants, coaches and facilitators to use the Values Perspectives theory and survey in their own practice. For more information on training or consulting services, contact Dr. Kenton Hyatt, khyatt@kairios.com.

The Values Perspectives Survey is available at values-perspectives.com.

About Kairios

Kairios, similarly to kairos, is an ancient Greek word meaning roughly, "being in the right place at the right time." The ancient Greeks envisioned the both the spiritual and practical essence of kairios by using an image similar to that of the archer familiar to students of Zen, whose attention is both focused and diffuse as she becomes one with the arrow, its flight, and the vital heart of the target. Another Greek image for kairios is that of the weaver who passes his shuttle between the ever-moving threads of the warp with the perfect timing born of holistically integrated rhythm to create something of beauty, organic strength and essential, practical utility.

CPSIA information can be obtained at www.ICGtesting.com
Printed in the USA
BVOW11s1127190614

356716BV00011B/786/P

9 780989 682756